Chat Room for Teens 2

Introduction

The Chat Room is a wonderful invention. It allows users instantly to communicate freely, and for free, with anyone in the world. They can talk about any subject they care to, and express their opinion in any way they like. They can even be in contact with many people at once. The Chat Room has indeed revolutionized global communication.

CHAT ROOM FOR TEENS operates in much the same way. English learners are encouraged to express themselves freely on a wide range of relevant topics. Many thought-provoking questions and examples are given to spur independent language usage. There are no specifically "right" or "wrong" answers, so there is no need for users to be intimidated — any more than if they were discussing the same topics in their own language instead of English. And this natural, interesting teaching method will build confidence as well as competence, helping the learners to master a skill that will have countless applications — social as well as commercial — around the world, for the rest of their lives.

English, after all, is actually Earthlish — if Dutch, Korean, Saudi, and Brazilian colleagues meet together in Moscow, they will undoubtedly talk to each other in English. And the ones who are best able to express themselves accurately and effortlessly will have a tremendous advantage over their less-talented fellows. Promoting this skill and facility in English is the goal and purpose of the entire line of LIS Korea books, from EXPRESS YOURSELF to TEEN TALK to any of the other fine publications by this thoughtful, progressive company.

Duane Vorhees

Contents

Chat Room for Teens 02

LESSON 11 Happy New Year!

Warm-up Dialog

Resolve Is Good

Barbara : New Year's Day is only a week away. Can you believe it, Bob?

Robert : It's hard to believe, Babs, but it's true. Another year is almost gone.

Barbara : Do you remember the New Year Resolutions you made last year?

Robert : Not really. I think I forgot them as soon as I made them.

Barbara : Well, I remember mine. And some of them actually came to pass.

Robert : Such as?

Barbara : Well, I said I would study harder. And my grades got better as a result.

Robert : Well, congratulations. But I remember one of your resolutions that you didn't keep.

Barbara : Which one is that?

Robert : I remember you said that you'd try to be kinder to your brother. But I think you're just as mean to me as you've ever been.

As life goes by, time seems to speed up. A month is like an hour, a year like a day.

Barbara : That's because you're such a rotten kid. Nobody could be kind to someone as bad as you.

Robert : That's exactly what I mean!

Barbara : But, seriously, what about this year? Are you making any resolutions?

Robert : Well, every year I promise to get more exercise and stop watching so much TV. So, I guess I'll try again this year.

Barbara : Well, good luck.

Robert : What about you? What is your new year's resolution?

Barbara : I'm going to try to do a better job keeping my promises.

Robert : That sounds like a good idea. You can start by promising to be nicer to me!

• Questions

1. Do you usually make new year's resolutions?
2. Do you make them by yourself or with the help of your parents or friends?
3. Make your next list of new year's resolutions now.

Pictures

1.

Q1: Do you feel happy when a new year begins? Why or why not?

Q2 What do you do on the first day of January?

Q3: Do you get a present from your parents? Or any special pocket money?

2.

Q1: Do you think time passes too fast? What makes you think so?

Q2 Do your parents say time is passing too fast or too slow? Does age make a difference?

Q3: Do you want to grow up soon? Why or why not?

3.

Q1: What were your most important new year's resolutions this year?

Q2 Do you always keep your resolutions? Why or why not?

Q3: What happens if you fail to keep them?

Talk

4. Q1: What were your parents' new year's resolutions this year?

Q2 Do you know if they kept them? What happened?

Q3: Why do you think it is usually hard to keep these resolutions?

5.

Q1: Do you like the teacher's resolutions? Why or why not?

Q2 What would you like your teachers to do for you and your friends?

Q3: Do you think your teachers really love you? Explain in detail.

6. Q1: What's the main difference between last year and this year?

Q2 Do you think you have a better understanding of your friends and family?

Q3: Do you feel more responsible towards your family and yourself?

LESSON 11 Happy New Year!

Answer Me

• 1 Negotiating a Raise

Randy : Hi, Mom. I want to talk to you about something important.

Mother : Certainly, son. What's on your mind?

Randy : Well, I think I need a bigger allowance.

Mother : Why? Don't you get enough?

Randy : It's okay, I guess. But I think I should get more because it's a new year.

Mother : Is that the only reason?

Randy : I guess so. But it's a pretty good reason!

Mother : Do you think your dad and I get a raise every year? Just because it's a new year?

Randy : I don't know. But you should!

Mother : Are you willing to do more work around the house? Help with chores?

Randy : Sure!

Mother : OK, I'll discuss it with your father when he comes home. We'll see what he says.

Randy : I'm sure he'll agree if you tell him you think it's a good idea.

Maybe I was happier with a small allowance and more free time.

• Questions

1. Do your parents increase your allowance every year?
2. Do you think you deserve a raise every year? Even if your own responsibilities remain the same?
3. What do you think a fair allowance would be for someone your age?

• 2 Overdoing It?

Mom : Charles, I think you're doing a wonderful job at school!

Charles : Thanks, Mom. But it isn't any better than usual. What's up?

Mom : I know I complain a lot when you do something wrong, so I decided that one of my new year's resolutions is to compliment you more. I don't want you to think I don't appreciate your accomplishments.

Charles : I don't think that.

Mom : I know you don't. You're so thoughtful!

Charles : I'm glad you think so.

Mom : And so appreciative!

Charles : Thanks, Mom. But it's kind of embarrassing when you act this way.

Mom : So humble!

Charles : Mom! Cut it out! I like it better when you're acting normal.

Mom : Don't you like compliments?

Charles : Sure, if I do something to deserve them. But not every second!

So insincere?

• Questions

1. Do you think adults usually keep their resolutions?
2. When do your parents praise you? When do they criticize you?
3. How do you feel when they complain about you? Do you ever think you deserve it?

LESSON 11 Happy New Year!

Answer Me

• 3 Promises, Promises

Ellen : Dad! I'm so disappointed in you. You promised to stop smoking!

Dad : I know I did. And I will. But right now I'm under a lot of stress from work. Smoking helps calm my nerves.

Ellen : But your job isn't any different than it always is, is it? How will next week be any different?

Dad : I just bought a new pack. If I don't smoke it all, it'll just be a waste of money.

Ellen : But a pack of cigarettes doesn't cost much. Bad health is a lot more expensive than that.

Dad : I know, but I bought it out of habit. I'm used to buying a pack when I buy a newspaper. I don't even think about doing it.

Ellen : I'll help you by just giving you enough change for a paper. That way you'll have to think about it.

Dad : Thanks, you're a big help. But smoking is also a habit. I've been smoking since I was in high school. It's hard to stop.

Ellen : But it would be easier if you actually tried to stop!

Dad : Okay. I promise.

Ellen : When?

Dad : Soon.

Promises are like money—
easier made than kept.

• Questions

1. To stop smoking is one of the most common new year's resolutions among adults. But many people fail. Can you explain why?
2. A lot of people suffer from secondhand smoke. What is that? Why is it a problem?
3. Do your parents smoke? If they do, could you get them to stop? How?

4 A Matter of Perspective

Jasmine : Don't you love it every time a new year comes?

Dad : No, not particularly.

Jasmine : But it's a time for starting over! I can get rid of all the bad things in my life and look forward to new challenges and adventures!

Dad : That's great. But you're young and have a lot to look forward to.

Jasmine : You're young, too!

Dad : Not any more. For me, a new year just means that I'm getting older. Each year that goes by means that I'm less and less likely to achieve my dreams. And everything costs more, just to keep what I already have.

Jasmine : Gosh, I hope that I never get so old that I feel that way.

Dad : I hope so, too.

Everybody wants to live a long time, but nobody wants to get old.

Questions

1. What do your parents think about the new year? Do they celebrate?
2. What does "everything costs more, just to keep what I already have" mean?
3. Is Jasmine's father a pessimist or an optimist? What about her? How about you?

LESSON 11 Happy New Year!

Let's Talk More

• 1 My New Year's Resolutions List

(1) I will study harder.
(2) I will exercise more.
(3) I will keep a balanced diet.
(4) I will find more time to help Mom and Dad.
(5) I will be kind to my brothers and sisters.
(6) I won't make any promise I don't think I can keep.
(7) I will be optimistic.
(8) I will turn off the TV one day a week.
(9) I won't trouble my parents to wake me up.
(10) I will read more books.

Is it better to have a thousand unattainable goals or a few that may be achieved?

• Questions

1. What is a "balanced diet"?
2. Do you help your mom or dad much? If so, how?
3. Are you always kind to your brothers and sisters? Are they kind to you? Why or why not?

2 My Resolutions

I have two ears but only one mouth. So I will listen more to my parents and teachers and try to do what they ask. And I will talk softly and not as much as I do now. I will volunteer more of my time to help others. I will apologize for my mistakes and forgive other people for their shortcomings. I will try to understand the viewpoints of others and especially why my parents and teachers nag me so much. And I won't make any lame excuses when I make a mistake.

You can win more friends with your ears than with your mouth.

Questions

1. Do you often volunteer your time for a good cause? If so, what do you do? If not, why not?
2. Do you always apologize when you think you made a mistake?
3. List three lame excuses that kids often make.

Let's Talk More

3 New Year's Resolutions My Parents Should Make

(1) I will treat my kids just like my friends.
(2) I will not get mad at them when they make mistakes.
(3) I will always cheer my kids up when they feel blue.
(4) I will raise their allowance and let them spend it on anything they like.
(5) When I'm stressed out, I won't take it out on my kids anymore.

In turn, if my parents keep all their promises above, I will respect them and follow their advice.

Questions

1. For each of the five resolutions, tell why your parents might disagree.
2. What would happen if you tried to apply them to your own parents? Would they work?
3. Make your own list of resolutions on behalf of your own parents.

• 4 How I Will Spend This Year

- In January, I will learn to ski.
- In February, I will visit my relatives in the United States.
- In March, I'll win a lot of money in the lottery.
- In April, I'll treat my friends and family to a big party and give them what they need most of all.
- In May, I'll find true love and decide who I will spend the rest of my life with.
- In June, I'll compose the greatest song ever written.
- In July, I'll invent a drug that can cure AIDS.
- In August, I'll bring my new American friends to my country to visit me.
- In September, I'll call the President and give him my plan for world peace.
- In October, I'll celebrate my birthday in Paris.
- In November, I'll master the newest on-line game.
- And in December, I'll make my plans for next year.

• Questions

1. How many of these plans do you think are likely to be achieved? Which ones?
2. Do you plan far ahead? What will you be doing next week? Next month? Next year? Ten years from now? Twenty-five years in the future?
3. What is your biggest goal this year?

LESSON 11 Happy New Year!

Real Talk

Should Be in the Proper Spirit

Mom : Carl, what are your new year's resolutions going to be?

Carl : I'm not going to make any this year.

Mom : Why not? You always make resolutions.

Carl : That's right. But they never work out.

Mom : What do you mean?

Carl : I try to keep them but always fail. I'm tired of living under the stress of failure, so I just won't make any.

Mom : I think that's the wrong attitude. You should try to improve yourself, even if you fail. If you don't succeed, you will have lost nothing, but you'll never do any better if you don't even try.

Carl : I suppose you're right.

Mom : Good! What are your resolutions, then?

Carl : Let me think.

Mom : Well?

Carl : OK. I'm going to try to be better at video games, and I'd like to get better grades without studying so hard.

What seems the best now might be the worst in the long term.

• Questions

1. Why did Carl decide not to make new year's resolutions?
2. Why does his mother think he should make some?
3. What is your opinion about his goals for the year?

Read Me

A Practical Approach

There is no tomorrow and no next year. Every day is the same as yesterday, and all years are alike. That's my attitude. That way nobody should ever make a big fuss about new year's resolutions. All we should ever have to worry about is doing our best today, not forever, and if we make a mistake this time, we'll just try again next time. And if today was wonderful, that does not mean tomorrow will be terrific as well, so we can't just rest on our laurels.

Newly Invented Calendar

There is no today! There is this second!

Questions

1. Do you agree with this attitude or not? Explain your answer.
2. Was today better than yesterday? How? Can you detect any improvement in anything, big or small?
3. In practical terms, what advice would you give to people to live happier lives?

Chat Room for Teens 02

LESSON 12 What Will You Do on Your Next Vacation?

Warm-up Dialog

The Beach? The Mountains? Or Elsewhere?

Pam : Wow! Summer's almost here! I can hardly wait for our vacation to start.

Dad : Where would you like to go this year? The beach or the mountains?

Pam : I don't want to stay here at all. I think we should travel abroad for once.

Dad : No, it's too expensive.

Pam : No, not really. A lot of my friends have gone to Europe or the US. They tell me that very inexpensive package deals are available all the time.

Dad : Really?

Pam : There's hardly any difference in price at all between staying home and going away.

Dad : I find that very hard to believe.

Pam : Why don't you look into it? I bet you'll be surprised at how little it costs to see Australia.

Dad : There are still lots of things here that you haven't seen yet. I think you should put your own country first, and then look around somewhere else later.

Pam : I can always travel around here. But, just once, I'd like to see how other people live. I think this would make me appreciate even more how great it is to be here.

Dad : OK, I'll look into it and see what it costs. But I think we'd better let your mom decide.

Pam : That sounds fair. I guess from now on I'll have to help her do a lot of housework.

Questions

1. What are the reasons Pam's dad wants to stay home?
2. How does Pam answer her father's concerns?
3. Why does Pam think she will have a lot of housework to do?

Pictures

1.

Q1: What is happening in the picture?

Q2 Do you worry about traffic when you go on vacation?

Q3: How can one avoid heavy traffic during the vacation season?

2.

Q1: What is happening in the picture?

Q2 Do you like to go swimming even when the pool is crowded? Why or why not?

Q3: What are some poolside safety precautions that should always be followed?

3.

Q1: Have you ever camped out? When and where?

Q2 What did you do there? Did you enjoy it?

Q3: What's the difference between staying in a condominium and in a tent? Which do you prefer? Why?

Talk

4. Q1: What do you do at the beach?

Q2 Do you like to tan? Why or why not?

Q3: What are good and bad things about going to the beach?

5.

Q1: Which do you like better, snow skiing or water skiing? Why?

Q2 Snow boarding and jet skiing are also popular. How do they compare with snow skiing and water skiing?

Q3: What other kinds of summer and winter activities can you think of?

6. Q1: Do you like to go hiking in the mountains? Why or why not?

Q2 What mountains have you climbed?

Q3: What do you think about rock climbing? Do you think it is easy or dangerous?

LESSON 12 What Will You Do on Your Next Vacation?

Answer Me

• 1 Chatting About Vacations

Jenny : hi. i'm glad i saw u on line. i wanted 2 tell u how much fun i'm having.

Dick : where r u?

Jenny : my family took a rafting trip. before we came, i was afraid, but now i know how much fun it is! i want to do it again!

Dick : maybe my fam will do it next yr. but this summer we go to the ocean.

Jenny : have u been there be4?

Dick : of course. many times. but this yr will be special.

Jenny : y?

Dick : cause dad says i'm going to learn how to surf. that really looks like fun!

Jenny : i tried last yr. i couldn't keep my balance. but it was fun anyhow.

Chatting online is just as personal as live contact, don't you think?

• Questions

1. Did you ever go rafting? Describe the experience. How about surfing?
2. What do you think the most interesting water sport is? Why?
3. Do you think Dick and Jenny are near each other? Why or why not?

2 Potential Problems

Andrew : Well, I'm definitely going to New York this summer. I'll spend my whole vacation staying with my uncle there.

Alice : Really! Aren't you excited?

Andrew : Part of me can't wait to go. I've always wanted to do this. But another part of me is kind of scared about going.

Alice : Why?

Andrew : I'm afraid my English isn't good enough. I won't be able to talk to anyone. Maybe I'll get lost or get in trouble because I don't understand something.

Alice : Don't worry! You can talk with your uncle, can't you?

Andrew : Sure. But that's just family. I want to talk to Americans to see what they think about things.

Alice : He'll take good care of you. But you know what our teacher says: You don't have to speak English perfectly to be understood! Don't worry about making mistakes, just do the best you can, and everything will be fine.

Questions

1. Have you ever visited any other countries? Where did you go?
2. What did you do there? Did you have language problems?
3. Where would you like to go?

LESSON 12 What Will You Do on Your Next Vacation?

Answer Me

3 A Long Walk

Mom : I signed you up to take a hike all across the country with the other Boy Scouts.

Tim : I wish you hadn't done that.

Mom : But we talked about this last week. I thought you wanted to do it.

Tim : I do. But I'm afraid it will be too hard. I don't know if I'm ready yet.

Mom : You're just as ready as anyone else. I'm sure you're anxious just because you've never done it before. But you'll be fine.

Tim : Do you really think so?

Mom : Of course. There will be plenty of experienced adults along in case there's a problem. But I wouldn't have signed you up if I thought you couldn't do it.

Questions

1. Do you think walking across your country would be a good experience? How long would it take?
2. What place in your country do you most want to visit?
3. How well do you think you know your own country? Have you visited every part?

4 A Different Destination

Britney : Are we going to the beach this summer?

Dad : No, I don't think so. We do that every year.

Britney : Then, we're going to the mountains instead?

Dad : No. This time we're going to do something different.

Britney : Stay home and relax?

Dad : No. I decided we'd do something useful this year. We're going someplace abroad where a typhoon has just struck, helping the victims rebuild and clean up.

Britney : What? What kind of holiday is that? Vacations are supposed to be fun!

Dad : Not everything in life is fun. Sometimes we need to think about other people and not just ourselves.

Questions

1. If you were Britney, what would you think about your father's plan?
2. Have you ever done any volunteer work? Describe the experience.
3. Talk about whether or not doing volunteer work is necessary.

LESSON 12 What Will You Do on Your Next Vacation?

Let's Talk More

1 At Different Times!

I hate to see everybody else taking a vacation at the same time in the summer as I do. The roads are crowded with cars, and the buses and trains are full. And all the popular places have too many people. I think the others should go some other time. If we all spread our vacations out over the whole year, we'd all have a better time.

Is it against the law to take a vacation in any season except summer?

Questions

1. Do you like to vacation in the summer? Why or why not?
2. Why don't people take their vacations in the spring or fall?
3. What time of year is the best for taking a vacation? Why?

2 The High Cost of Having Fun

I can't understand why everything is more expensive during the holidays. Lodging expenses are through the roof, and meal prices are outrageous. At the same time, fuel costs are skyrocketing. People are so angry about this that maybe everyone will start staying at home during vacation time.

Why are they going up and up now?
We can't go on vacation until they start to go down.

Questions

1. Do you think things are more expensive during holiday seasons? Why?
2. How do you feel when you get ripped off?
3. What can people do to avoid being overcharged?

Let's Talk More

• 3 Who Wins?

My family can't agree on anything. Dad wants to visit his parents. My sister wants to go to the beach. I want to go abroad. And Mom just wants to stay home. She says it is more convenient, less crowded, and cheaper, and that we can enjoy many things without going very far.

We should go our separate ways and just forget about taking a FAMILY trip.

• Questions

1. Which one do you agree with most? Why?
2. How would you persuade your family to agree with you?
3. In your family, who usually decides how to spend your vacation? Do you always agree?

4 My Weird Brother

My brother is very odd. He wants to stay at home during summer vacation! He says he likes to stay in his own air conditioned house, and at home he can eat whenever he wants and play video games and watch movies any time he likes. But if he goes somewhere, he doesn't have any friends to enjoy himself with, and he gets bored and uncomfortable very easily. He's a real stick-in-the-mud!

I don't think I'm weird!
I think everyone else is strange.

Questions

1. Do you understand the brother? Do you agree or disagree with him? Why?
2. What would happen if everyone stayed at home all the time? What if nobody ever stayed at home?
3. Does everyone always like the same things? Give some examples.

LESSON 12 What Will You Do on Your Next Vacation?

Real Talk

12 Countries in 14 Days

Keith : Hi! How are you?

Carol : I'm fine. Where were you yesterday? I thought we were supposed to meet.

Keith : Yes, we were. But I fell asleep. I was exhausted from my trip, and I guess I'm still suffering from jet lag. I'm sorry.

Carol : Where did you go?

Keith : My whole family spent two weeks in Europe.

Carol : What did you see?

Keith : Everything, I think! We spent a lot of time on buses and guided tours, but we saw 12 different countries. I had no idea how different from each other they all are!

Carol : Twelve countries in 2 weeks! No wonder you're tired.

Keith : We saw a bull fight in Spain. But I don't understand why people get so excited about it. Mostly, it was just very boring. A good action movie is lots more exciting than that.

Carol : Did you go to Paris or Florence? Did you see the museums there?

Keith : My parents went, but I was allowed to skip the Louvre. Why would anyone want to waste a whole day looking at old statues and paintings?

Carol : Then, what was the high point of the trip?

Keith : Oh, I guess going to Switzerland. The Alps were awesome!

Carol : I wish I could go someday. But I think I'd like to spend most of my time in one place and get to know it well, rather than spend the entire vacation going from one place to another.

Keith : Next year, maybe we'll just go to Australia. We probably won't travel so much there.

Carol : Haven't you looked at a map? Australia is an enormous place. The whole continent is only one country! I bet things are even farther apart than in Europe.

Time is money! Quick! Quick! Quick!

Questions

1. Why did Keith miss his appointment yesterday?
2. What was the favorite part of his vacation?
3. Do you think Carol would enjoy an American package tour — that went to many places over a short period of time? Why or why not?

Read Me

Two Types of Traveler

Tourists are the same the world over. They want new experiences, but they also want to take part of their comfort zone with them. I guess this is why Americans eagerly visit their familiar fast-food restaurants wherever they go, and why it is so difficult for Koreans to go anyplace that doesn't serve kimchi. Some tourists insist on staying in first-class hotels and having their entire itineraries planned for them in advance. It seems they are mostly interested in having their photographs taken in front of a famous place and buying tee shirts to prove to their skeptical friends they have actually been there. Then they want to go to the next hot spot on the map and repeat the process all over again, until it is finally time to return home. Other tourists are the classic back-packers. They spend as little money as possible and take an adventurous delight in discovering the unexpected. They may spend weeks being dirty and uncomfortable, but they treasure the authenticity of their travel. However, cheap hotels and youth hostels tend to be depressingly alike in every country, and the best things to be experienced abroad are not necessarily free.

• Questions

1. What are the two kinds of tourists, according to the essay?
2. In what ways are most tourists the same?
3. Which kind of tourist would you rather be? Why?

Chat Room for Teens 02

LESSON 13 Adults Are Too Busy

Warm-up Dialog

Busy, Busy, Busy

Lulu : Do you really know any adults?

Jeremy : Sure. My parents.

Lulu : No. I mean do you really know them? How much time do you spend with them?

Jeremy : Well, not much, I guess. If I ask them to play a game with me, they say they're too busy.

Lulu : I know what you mean. When I ask them to help me with my homework, they say, "I don't have time."

Jeremy : My parents are even too busy to spend time with each other. They exercise separately and eat at different times.

Lulu : Do your parents ever even talk with each other?

Even in the car, they are busy!
Are they on the phone in their sleep, too?

Jeremy : Not that I'm aware of!

Lulu : When my folks get home late, they've usually been drinking, and they go directly to bed.

Jeremy : If I get home late, Mom usually isn't there, so I have to fix my own meal.

Lulu : Do your parents ever make excuses for being so busy?

Jeremy : They tell me they have to work so hard for the family that they don't have any time to spend with us.

Lulu : I feel sorry for them.

Jeremy : Yeah. I bet they'd feel better if they actually got to relax with us and have some fun.

• Questions

1. What's the biggest problem adults have, according to Jeremy's parents?
2. What are the main excuses they give?
3. What could they do to solve the problem?

Pictures

1.

Q1: Does your father work a lot? What about your mom?

Q2 What time does your father usually come home?

Q3: How often does your father say "I'm too busy" or "I'm too tired"?

2.

Q1: Do you think adults spend a lot of time taking care of their parents? What makes you think so?

Q2 Do you think adults spend much time taking care of their kids? Why do you think that way?

Q3: Despite what they say, do you think they mostly just take care of themselves? Explain your answer.

3.

Q1: Adults always claim to be busy. But they always make time to enjoy themselves. What do you think about that?

Q2 Why do you think so many adults smoke and drink so much?

Q3: Do you believe they smoke and drink because of their jobs or for some other reason? Explain your answer.

Talk

4\. Q1: Whom do adults usually have to meet? Why?

Q2 Do you usually stay at home when your parents go out to meet somebody? How do you feel then?

Q3: Which do you think is more important, parents meeting somebody else or playing with their kids?

5\.

Q1: Do your parents play golf? Why or why not? How often?

Q2 Do you think playing golf is expensive or cheap? How much does it cost?

Q3: What sports do your parents enjoy?

6\. Q1: Do you think adults really are always busy with their kids? Why or why not?

Q2 How often do your parents make time to play, study, or talk with you?

Q3: Some kids are left alone with no parental care. Why?

LESSON 13 Adults Are Too Busy

Answer Me

• 1 Hard at Work

Laura : Dad.

Dad : Mmmmmmmm.

Laura : Dad!

Dad : What?

Laura : I need some help with my homework.

Dad : Right now I'm busy. I'll help you later.

Laura : What are you doing?

Dad : I'm working.

Laura : But you're just watching television!

Dad : No, I'm not. I'm working in my mind. I have a problem at work that I have to solve, and I'm thinking about it.

Laura : When will you be ready to help me?

Dad : As soon as the football game is over.

Maybe the problem at work is his poor golf scores.

• Questions

1. Do you believe Laura's father? Why or why not?
2. What would you do if you were in Laura's situation?
3. Which should be more important, Father's work or Laura's homework?

• 2 Passing The Buck

Ryan : Mom. I need you.

Mom : OK, OK. But right now I can't. I have something to do.

Ryan : Yes, I know how busy you are. You're always busy shopping and gossiping with your friends on the phone.

Mom : But I'm not too busy to spank my disrespectful son.

Ryan : I'm sorry, Mom. But I need your help. I have a science project that I'm having trouble with.

Mom : Can you get your dad to help you? He's better in science than I am.

Ryan : I already asked him. He told me he was too busy, so I should ask you.

• Questions

1. Does your mom work outside the home? What does she do?
2. What keeps your mom busy most of the time? How does she spend her time?
3. Do you think most women talk a lot? How about men?

LESSON 13 Adults Are Too Busy

Answer Me

• 3 Parentless Part-Time

Roy : Did you ever feel like an orphan?

Janice : Of course not, silly! Both of my parents are still alive.

Roy : So are mine, but I never see them on weekends.

Janice : Why not?

Roy : I don't know. But they always tell me they have something to do, and I spend all weekend home alone.

Janice : Don't you ever get to go with them?

Roy : No, never.

Janice : What about the rest of the week?

Roy : Well, Mom's always home, and Dad comes in from work early every day. So then I don't feel like I'm by myself.

Janice : I guess you really are a "weekend orphan," then.

Some other kids think he's lucky, since he's alone only on weekends but they are by themselves all the time.

• Questions

1. Do your parents spend time with you on weekends?
2. What do you usually do together?
3. Do you really enjoy being with your parents? Or would you rather spend more time with your friends? Explain your answer.

• 4 Never Too Late

Henrietta : Dad, what are you doing?

Dad : I'm studying English.

Henrietta : Why? You aren't in school anymore. You graduated a long time ago.

Dad : A person doesn't have to be in school in order to need to study.

Henrietta : But why?

Dad : Everyone has to learn new skills and meet new challenges. And, besides, it can be fun.

Henrietta : I don't ever think it's fun.

Dad : Well, I guess I felt that way too when I was your age. Maybe that's why I have to study English now. If I had studied it well when I was a kid, it wouldn't be so hard for me to learn now.

Henrietta : But why do you need it now?

Dad : I have a chance for a big promotion. But I have to be fluent in English to get it. So I have to study hard!

Learning lasts from the cradle to the grave.

• Questions

1. Do your parents ever study English? Why or why not?
2. Do they ever study anything? What?
3. Do they think English is difficult? Why is English so different from your own language?

LESSON 13 Adults Are Too Busy

Let's Talk More

1 Many Responsibilities

I understand that adults are busy. For instance, both of my parents work. And they still have a family to support and a home to look after. They also have to plan on taking care of themselves even after they stop working. Traditionally, kids have supported their parents when they get old, but my parents are afraid that modern kids won't do that anymore. I tell them not to worry, but they say they don't want to take any chances.

Too much life baggage to carry easily.

Questions

1. Do you think your parents have a hard time supporting you?
2. Do your parents want you to take care of them after they retire? How do you feel about that?
3. If you can't support them when they get old, what would they do?

• 2 The Usual Answer

I don't believe that adults are as busy as they claim to be. It seems to me that they can always find the time to do whatever they like. They just pretend to be busy when I need them to do something with me. Then, all I hear is, "Later," or "Not right now." If I ask why, they just say "I'm busy!"

The answer is not ALWAYS the same, but the meaning is.

• Questions

1. Why are parents busy?
2. Do you know why adults say "I'm busy" so often? What is your opinion?
3. Are kids busier than adults or less busy, do you think?

LESSON 13 Adults Are Too Busy

Let's Talk More

• 3 Busy Too!

Teenagers are busy too, you know. They have to study a lot of boring subjects in school, and then after school they still have to study something else, like piano or English. But the adults never realize how busy their kids are and think that they are the only ones who are really busy! I wish I really did have as much free time to be with my friends as my parents seem to think I have!

• Questions

1. Are you busy? What do you do?
2. Do your parents know that you are busy? Do they ever do anything to help you relax? What?
3. Who is busier, do you think, you, your mother, or your father? Who has the most fun in life?

• 4 How Do They Do It?

I respect my parents. They are always ready to learn something new and willing to correct themselves if they are wrong. They keep reading books and thinking. They even write down their thoughts in a journal. They are never idle, even when they are at home relaxing. And they still find plenty of time to spend with me. I hope I'm like that when I grow up.

Studying doesn't end with finishing school.

• Questions

1. Are your parents ever idle? When?
2. What do your parents do when they have free time?
3. What are your parents studying these days, if anything? What about you?

LESSON 13 Adults Are Too Busy

Real Talk

The New Division of Labor

Dad : It's been a long day. I'm going to watch a football game on TV.

Harold : Me, too.

Juliet : I don't like football, but I'll gladly watch it with you. How about you, Mom?

Mom : I'd love to! But, unfortunately, I'm not finished yet. While the three of you are relaxing after "a long day," I'm still working. That doesn't seem very fair to me.

Dad : I think you kids should help your mother.

Mom : What about you? Are you going to be the only one in this household who gets waited on hand and foot?

Dad : Oh, I didn't mean that I wasn't going to help too. What do you want me to do?

Mom : Why don't you clean the bathroom? Every week!

Dad : OK, it's a deal. Harold, why don't you vacuum the floor?

Juliet : I'll do the dishes.

Mom : Good. I'm glad you're all taking me seriously for a change.

Harold : While we're doing our chores, what are you going to do?

Mom : I think I'll watch that football game you mentioned.

Turnabout is fair play.

Questions

1. What are the kids and their dad planning to do?
2. Why doesn't their mother think this is fair?
3. What solution is decided on? Is it fair?

Read Me

Who's the Busiest?

Why are people so busy? Does life have to be that way? Before the so-called "labor-saving devices" became available, people were more productive and yet had more time to relax. Novelists who had to write and revise by hand were more prolific, and had more to say, than modern ones, who use word processors to do most of their work. Without mechanical equipment and chemical fertilizers, farmers planted more acreage, and the food was more varied and healthier than now. But today, we can do "two things at once," so our employers, our parents, and our teachers expect us to do so all the time. After a while, we take it for granted that we're supposed to be multi-tasking. But we are generally less satisfied with our work output, because it has become such an impersonal process, and its quality is also probably worse due to a lack of loving attention given to the fine details. Adults like to complain about how busy they are, but I know I start school before my parents go to work, and I'm not finished until after they both get back home. So, if being busy means the amount of time spent doing what someone else wants one to do, instead of the time spent working on one's own private affairs, then I guess kids are the busiest people there are.

Questions

1. How would you define "busy"? According to that definition, how busy are you?
2. If you spend a lot of time on your hobbies or playing with your friends, does that count as being "busy"?
3. Some adults make enough money and have plenty of time to relax, while others are always busy but make a little money. What's the difference between them?

LESSON 14 Emergency

Warm-up Dialog

Should We Worry?

Mom : Did you feel that earthquake last night?

Jake : What earthquake?

Mom : Oh, it was nothing, really. The bed was shaking, that's all. You must have slept right through it.

Jake : What time did that happen?

Mom : About midnight, I guess.

Jake : It's strange, but yesterday we talked about earthquakes in Science class.

Having high numbers is not necessarily good.

Mom : What a coincidence!

Jake : Yeah. The teacher said there are quakes every day, but we don't notice them because they are so slight.

Mom : I'm surprised to hear that. I thought last night was an unusual event.

Jake : But it could have been a lot worse. We all could have been killed instantly, and we never would have known about it.

Mom : Oh, don't worry about it. Those big ones really are very rare.

Jake : But they can happen anywhere, and we don't have any way of predicting where or when.

Mom : So, there isn't any reason to worry about it if there isn't anything we can do about it, is there?

Jake : No, that's all the more reason to worry. If we had more control, we could worry less.

• Questions

1. What happened last night? Who knew about the quake, Jake or his mother?
2. Should we worry more about earthquakes, or less?
3. Do you know what to do in case of an earthquake?

Pictures

1.

Q1: What is happening in the picture? Has your house ever been broken into?

Q2 What do burglars usually steal?

Q3: What punishment do you think burglars deserve?

2.

Q1: What is happening here?

Q2 What did the boy do wrong?

Q3: What would you do if you saw this happen in real life?

3.

Q1: What is happening in the picture?

Q2 What should you do if someone were seriously sick and there was no one there to help you?

Q3: Have you ever gone to an emergency room? What happened?

Talk

4. Q1: What happened here? What should you do if you were one of the drivers?

Q2 What are the main causes of traffic accidents?

Q3: Is your family car insured? What does it mean to be insured?

5.

Q1: What is happening? Have you ever seen a house on fire?

Q2 What do you think about firefighters?

Q3: What does "arson" mean? Do you have any idea why firebugs behave as they do?

6. Q1: What in the world is happening?

Q2 Does it flood often where you live?

Q3: Who should be responsible for the damage, the government or the people?

LESSON 14 Emergency

Answer Me

1 Watch Out!

Karen : Are you all right? You look pale.

Paul : I just came back from the hospital.

Karen : Oh! What happened?

Paul : I burned myself in hot water.

Karen : Oh! That's terrible.

Paul : I was playing with my brother in the kitchen and bumped against the stove. A pan of hot water fell on me.

Karen : Are you OK?

Paul : I was lucky. The water wasn't quite boiling yet. So the doctors put some salve on my hand and told me I'd be OK.

Karen : Next time be more careful!

Why didn't anybody ever tell me boiling water is so hot???!!!!!!

Questions

1. Have you ever been burned or scalded?
2. Do you know how to treat a scald? What do you do in case of a burn?
3. What are the best ways to avoid being burned or scalded?

• 2 Be More Careful

Francis : Owwwwwwwww!

Mom : Frank! What's wrong!

Francis : I think I cut myself.

Mom : You're bleeding! Let me look!

Francis : It hurts!

Mom : I don't think it's too bad. Let's see if we can stop the bleeding.

Francis : I think it stopped now.

Mom : Let's just squeeze here a little longer to be sure. Then we'll wash it very thoroughly and see if you need stitches.

Francis : No, I think it's OK. I was surprised when I cut myself, but I don't really think it's a bad cut.

Mom : You need to be careful when you're holding a knife.

• Questions

1. Do you ever peel an apple or a pear by yourself?
2. Have you ever had a paper cut?
3. What should you do to keep from cutting yourself?

Answer Me

3 An Unpleasant Occurrence

Wasps are small, but their sting is large.

Victor : Ouch!

Valerie : What happened?

Victor : I just got stung by a wasp!

Valerie : Oh! Where is it now?

Victor : I swatted at it, but it flew away.

Valerie : Good! I hope it isn't here anymore. I don't want to get stung too!

Victor : No, it's gone.

Valerie : How do you feel?

Victor : It hurts! And it's starting to swell up.

Valerie : I think we need to go home and get it treated.

Victor : Yes, I think you're right. Let's go.

Valerie : Do you need any help?

Victor : No, I think I'll be okay until we get home.

Valerie : Mom told us to watch out for snakes and insects.

Victor : Yeah. Now I know why. It really hurts!

Questions

1. Have you ever been stung by a wasp or some other insect?
2. When you are in the woods, are you afraid of snakes?
3. Do you know how to avoid getting bitten by wild animals?

4 Helping a Lost Child

Bernice : Who's that up ahead?

Augie : It looks like a little kid. I've never seen him before.

Bernice : Why is he crying?

Augie : Maybe he's lost. Little boy, do you know where your parents are?

Bernice : I think he's too little to talk.

Augie : Maybe we can get him to stop crying.

Bernice : Then we can try to find his parents.

Questions

1. What has happened?
2. What should Augie and Bernice do?
3. Have you ever been lost alone in a strange place? How were you found?

Let's Talk More

1 Thunderstruck!

Have you ever been wakened in the middle of the night by a thunderstorm? Have you tried counting the seconds between a lightning flash and the sound of thunder to find out how far away the lightning is? The sound of thunder is a very dramatic and sometimes frightening event. Throughout history, and around the world, it has inspired people to create stories about it. For instance, the ancient Germans told many tales about Thor, the God of Thunder, while the Greeks and Romans usually pictured their chief god (Zeus or Jupiter) with a thunderbolt in his hand.

Questions

1. Are you scared of thunderstorms?
2. What are the precautions you should take if you are outside during a thunderstorm?
3. Do you know any stories (myths, fairy tales) about what causes thunder?

• 2 Lucky or Careful — Which is Better?

Most accidents are preventable. People generally know how to avoid them. But we are too cocksure and unconcerned to take sufficient care. That is why we disobey traffic laws; we run with scissors in our hands; we don't read warning labels on appliances: we don't think anything bad can happen to us. And most of the time, we get away with it; nothing happens, everything is fine; and so next time we do the same careless thing. But, eventually, sooner or later, our lack of attention catches up with us, and we get hurt or we injure someone else. Only then do we think about the consequences of our poor behavior — but, then, it is too late.

• Questions

1. Why do people drown?
2. Why are there so many fires?
3. Why are there so many injuries due to car accidents?

Let's Talk More

3 Suddenly!

One of the most frightening natural occurrences in the world is a tsunami. It comes without warning. There is no sound. The sky does not suddenly become dark. The earth doesn't shake. And it may be caused by a geological event that occurred thousands of miles away, perhaps deep under water. But, suddenly, a massive amount of water comes upon us all at once and carries away everything in its path. People drown and buildings are knocked down. Cars and buses are overturned and roads swept away. And then as quickly as it came, it is gone, leaving a path of destruction behind.

The weatherman sure missed this one!

Questions

1. Where do tsunamis usually take place? When?
2. What happens when a tsunami occurs?
3. How are they caused? Do they happen often?

• 4 The Policy

Insurance is a simple idea, really. Several people are concerned about some kind of potential catastrophe, let's say a house fire. They know that the odds against their own particular homes burning down are remote, but they also know that if it happens they can't recover their losses very easily. So they all agree to pool some resources and use the collective money to pay for fire damage to any of their homes. The odds against it happening remain the same, but now if one of them gets unlucky at least he won't lose everything.

• Questions

1. Is your house insured against fire?
2. Is your family's car insured? What does the insurance cover?
3. Are your parents' lives insured? What about your life?

LESSON 14 Emergency

Real Talk

Red Is Red, Not Pink

Ryan : Look at that car!

Mom : Yes, I see it. I wondered why the traffic was moving so slowly. I thought there must be an accident, and there it is!

Ryan : There's only one car. What happened?

Mom : They must have already towed the other one away. It looks like that one was broadsided. Probably the other driver ran a red light and hit this one.

Ryan : Do you think anyone was hurt?

Mom : It's hard to say. The windshield is not smashed. I'd guess the driver of this car was wearing a seat belt and is probably OK. But I wonder how bad the other car looked before they took it away.

Ryan : Driving is scary.

Mom : You get used to it. But you have to be very alert all the time.

Ryan : If this guy was going through a green light and was halfway across the intersection before he was rammed by someone running a red light, how could he have avoided the accident?

Mom : Well, that's right. We can't always be sure we're safe, no matter what we do. But most of the time we'll be fine if we're careful and we try to anticipate what the cars around us are going to do. And not be in too much of a hurry.

Ryan : You sound like Dad!

Mom : Your father's a smart man!

• Questions

1. What do you think caused the accident?
2. What are some good driving rules?
3. A good driver is one who, after seeing a wreck, drives carefully for several blocks. What does this mean?

Read Me

I'd Rather Not Think About It

We think we are great, but actually we are midgets compared to Nature. We are powerless in many natural disasters. They can happen suddenly, at any time, and destroy our lives. However, we can diminish our losses and survive even dreadful misfortunes such as earthquakes, typhoons, etc. We know how to make buildings that are strong enough and flexible enough to withstand these accidents. We can make dams to protect us against floods. Many of these terrible events are predictable. Heavy rains occur in the same places every year. We know when hurricanes are most likely, and with satellites we watch them as the storms build and move. And we know how to behave when these natural tragedies occur. So we are not entirely helpless. But most of us prefer to believe that "it can't happen to me" and fail to take even elementary precautions.

By obeying Mother Nature, we can command her.

Questions

1. How great are we, really?
2. What can happen to us?
3. How can we prevent some of the bad consequences of natural disasters?
4. Why don't we?

Chat Room for Teens 02

LESSON 15 Everybody Is Different

Warm-up Dialog

I.Q. Is Not Everything

Paula : What's wrong? You look depressed.

Paul : I just got my test results back. I didn't do very well in math at all, and not as well as I thought I would in my other subjects. I wish I were more like Fred; he got almost perfect scores in everything.

Paula : Well, Fred might be smart, but isn't a very nice guy. There's nothing wrong with being intelligent, but that's not the only thing that matters.

Paul : You're just saying that. I bet your scores were pretty good too!

Paula : They could be better, but I'm not ashamed of them. But they don't tell the whole story of who I am.

Everyone is gifted in different ways. We need to discover and develop our own talents.

Paul : But my parents expect a lot out of me. I don't want to disappoint them by being a failure.

Paula : Who says you're a failure? You're the most popular kid in our class. You're kind and outgoing, a lot more so than Fred!

Paul : But that isn't good enough. I want to go to college.

Paula : You don't have to be a great scholar to get a college degree, you know. For instance, you're a gifted athlete and a talented musician. There are lots of valuable skills that exist, and nobody has a monopoly on them all.

Paul : Well, you certainly have a gift for making people feel better about themselves. Thank you!

Paula : Don't mention it. Sometime when I'm feeling blue, you can return the favor.

Questions

1. Why is Paul sad?
2. What gifts does he have (at least three)?
3. Describe Fred.

Pictures

1.

Q1: Do you prefer studying during the day or night?

Q2 Are you a night owl or an early bird?

Q3: What about your parents?

2.

Q1: Do you think you are tall, short, or of average height?

Q2 What do you think would be your ideal height? Why?

Q3: Are you envious of your friends who are taller than you? Why or why not?

3.

Q1: Do you want to be rich? Why or why not?

Q2 Do you know how to become rich? What is the recipe?

Q3: What would you do if you were rich?

Talk

4\.

Q1: Do your parents always obey the traffic rules? Which ones do they break most often, if any?

Q2 Do you scold your parents if they break the law? What happens then?

Q3: List the rules you think adults break most often. Which ones do kids break?

5\.

Q1: Describe your parents. Are they silent or talkative? What else can you say about their personalities?

Q2 What about you? Are you talkative? What do you talk about the most?

Q3: What do you think about your friends? Which ones do you like better, the ones who are talkative or silent? Why?

6\.

Q1: Define "optimist" and "pessimist."

Q2 Describe yourself. Are you an optimist or a pessimist? Why do you think so?

Q3: Talk about the merits and demerits of being an optimist or a pessimist.

LESSON 15 Everybody Is Different

Answer Me

1 Pet Friends

Mort : Do you like animals?

Renee : No! I can't stand them.

Mort : Why not?

Renee : I don't like the way little dogs bark and snap at strangers. I'm afraid!

Mort : They're too little to hurt you. The noise is all bluff because they're so harmless.

Renee : Cats are even worse. They always look like they're trying to analyze you. It gives me the creeps.

Mort : Well, what about snakes and lizards? I have a bunch of them at home. Do you want to see them?

Questions

1. Do you like pets? Why or why not? What do your parents think?
2. What kind of pets would you like to have? What do you think about having rare animals as pets, such as spiders or lizards?
3. Talk about the responsibilities pet people have to their neighbors.

2 Play or Read?

Mac : Let's go outside! We can play basketball.

Nadine : No, I want to stay indoors and finish a mystery I'm reading.

Mac : But you can do that by yourself, any time!

Nadine : OK. But let's play a computer game instead. I don't want to get sweaty.

Not one without the other!

Questions

1. Do you like sports or books better?
2. What about your friends? Do they play ball a lot? Or do they study a lot?
3. Do your parents want you to study or play? Is that fair?

LESSON 15 Everybody Is Different

—— Answer Me ——

3 Mutual Envy

Maurice : I'm jealous.

Darlene : Of what?

Maurice : Of you! You're so bright! You even take a class with college students, and I have to struggle just to pass my high school courses. I wish I were as intelligent as you.

Darlene : Well, thank you for the compliment. But sometimes I wish I were like you! You're always so straightforward and honest. I could never come up to people and tell them how I feel, like you do.

Questions

1. Do you think you are gifted or ordinary? What makes you think so?
2. Do you wish you were more gifted? What talents would you especially like to have?
3. Do you think gifted people are happy? Why or why not?

• 4 Meatless

Barry : Thanks for having lunch with me.

Mary : Think nothing of it. It's my pleasure.

Barry : I'm going to have the pork cutlet. How about you?

Mary : I can't. I'm a vegetarian.

Barry : Are you a vegan?

Mary : No. I drink milk and eat eggs. Sometimes I even eat fish. But I never eat meat.

Barry : Why not?

Mary : Even thinking about it makes me sick to my stomach.

• Questions

1. Do you like meat? What is your favorite?
2. Do you like vegetables? What is your favorite? Which ones do you like the least?
3. Do you know any vegetarians? Do they seem healthy or unhealthy?

LESSON 15 Everybody Is Different

Let's Talk More

• 1 Opposite Personalities

Introverts are people who are more reserved than others. They are usually thought of as being bookworms or loners. Very few people know them well, but they often have very intense relationships with their close friends. Extroverts, on the other hand, are unusually outgoing. They are very talkative and are considered the life of any party. Though widely popular, however, they may not have deep friendships.

• Questions

1. Talk about your friends who are outgoing. Do you like to be with them? Are you comfortable in their presence?
2. Do you have any friends who are introverts? How do they behave? What do you do together?
3. Describe your own character.

2 Obedience or Revolution?

Some kids are rebellious against their teachers or parents, and others are very obedient. Much can be said about both kinds. The rebels challenge authority and may be agents of future change, but they cause a lot of trouble and pain, and they also suffer a lot of punishment. Many times, their actions are selfish, undisciplined, and self-defeating. On the other hand, the obedient, well-behaved kids provide social stability. Most of them will have productive jobs and be positive role models for others. But they are not likely to rock many boats to make the world a better place.

I don't understand why he wants to tear down authority. At my house, I get everything I want!

Questions

1. Do you think you are mainly rebellious or obedient?
2. Do you think kids should obey their parents and teachers under all circumstances?
3. What does "rock the boat" mean? What happens if someone rocks the boat too hard?

Let's Talk More

3 Three Generations

Meet Willie. He's a good kid who loves his father very much and wants his dad to be proud of him. But Willie's father, who loves Willie very much, is also very impatient and hot-tempered. He is never satisfied with Willie's accomplishments or behavior. There is a lot of tension between the two. But Willie's grandfather is very understanding. He gently encourages Willie to do better. Willie doesn't understand why his father is angry with him so often, and he wonders how his grandfather and his dad got along when his dad was growing up.

The middle generation is always isolated.

Questions

1. Describe your parents. Are they patient with you? Do they always understand you?
2. Describe your grandparents. Do they always seem to sympathize with you?
3. Who would you rather grow up with, your parents or grandparents?

• 4 Not Begging for Happiness

I see Old Bill again. He's a street beggar. I see him here on this corner almost every day. He lost both his legs when he was just a boy. His clothes are worn and ragged, and I don't think he has a family to go home to. But, nonetheless, he seems content. He's always smiling, and he knows most of the people around here by name. I often wonder how anyone can be so happy even with no money and no job.

Steady salary and good benefits — but why doesn't anybody major in panhandling?

• Questions

1. Do you think the rich are always happy? Why?
2. Do you think the poor can be happy too? Why?
3. Is it possible that some panhandlers are not really poor — that they actually make a lot of money on their "job"?

LESSON 15 Everybody Is Different

Real Talk

Are Looks Everything?

Father : What a wonderful movie that was! I feel so much better now, after seeing it.

Eileen : Not me. I feel much worse.

Father : How can that be? It had such a satisfying, uplifting ending.

Eileen : But the star! She's so beautiful. I look really plain in comparison.

Father : Who says so? I think you're very attractive.

Eileen : Dad! You're my father! You're supposed to say that!

Father : But it's true.

Eileen : I think I need a face lift. And maybe a boob job, too.

Father : Don't be silly. Plastic surgery is fine for extreme cases, like after a disfiguring accident or fire, but it's over rated otherwise. It's just a waste of money—my money!

Eileen : But, Dad, if I looked better I'd be more popular, and I'd have a better chance at getting a rich husband.

Father : You're too young to be worried about getting married. And you look just fine the way you are.

Eileen : But only "just fine," not "gorgeous."

Father : Look, beauty is entirely in the eye of the beholder. The actress you saw isn't so hot, actually, by my standards. She's too skinny, and her mouth is too big. There is no absolute definition of "beautiful." Everyone looks different, and people have different opinions about what beauty means.

Eileen : That's easy for you to say. You're already middle-aged and married, so being good looking doesn't matter much to you. But it's important to me! I have to compete with a lot of girls who are better looking than I am. If you don't get me plastic surgery, you'll be responsible for my spending my life with some other loser, because nobody else will want me.

Father : My, my. Aren't we melodramatic!

• Questions

1. Describe what makes a person beautiful. (At least five characteristics.)
2. Who is the most beautiful woman you know? The most handsome man?
3. Is physical beauty the most important aspect of being popular? Explain your answer in detail.

Read Me

What a Happy Life Is

People have different viewpoints about what a happy life is. If someone is not rich, he may think that money is the most important aspect in achieving happiness (because he has little of it). But he may also believe that other things are more important, in the long run. For example, family and friendship may be the most valuable parts of anyone's life; without these, it really doesn't matter how rich one is. If a girl is not satisfied with her looks, she can develop other traits to overcome that lack; she can have a kind smile and concentrate on having a positive outlook on life. Many handicapped people are actually happier than most others are, because they have learned to put their situation in clearer perspective; what they actually have is often more valuable to them than what they do not aspire unsuccessfully to get.

Life is a deck of cards with many possibilities for happiness.

Questions

1. What makes a person the happiest?
2. Do you think you are a happy person? What would make you happier?
3. Who's the happiest person you know? What makes him or her so happy?

Chat Room for Teens 02

LESSON 16 No Buts!

Warm-up Dialog

A Start

Rebecca : Dad! I thought you were going to stop smoking. I'm very disappointed in you.

Dad : I know, I know. I'm trying.

Rebecca : And you promised to cut down on your drinking, too. Have you done that?

Dad : Oh, I think I have, a little. But it's hard to quit all at once.

Rebecca : You know I love you. These habits are terrible! I want you around for a long time, that's why I want you to take better care of yourself.

If it weren't for my job, I wouldn't have any bad habits.

Dad : Drinking and smoking are hard habits to break, but I'm trying. But I have to go out with clients and with my fellow workers, and we always end up going to a bar. In those circumstances, I have to drink and smoke, too. I can't help it.

Rebecca : Well, you're not at a bar now. You're home!

Dad : I know! But it's not easy. But I'll put out this cigarette right now. And I won't smoke another one tonight. How's that?

Rebecca : That's good! But I'll be watching you!

• Questions

1. What is Rebecca's concern?
2. What are her father's excuses?
3. Does he try to cooperate with Rebecca? How?

Pictures

1\.

Q1: What are the most common excuses for being late for school?

Q2 What are the actual reasons for being late? Are they the same as the excuses?

Q3: What does your teacher do if you or your friend is late?

2\.

Q1: Do you like doing homework? Why or why not?

Q2 Does your teacher give you a lot of homework? Do you always do it all?

Q3: If you don't do your homework, what will your teacher do?

3\.

Q1: Do you have a curfew?

Q2 Do you ever stay out late? Why?

Q3: Are your parents angry if you come home late?

Talk

4\. Q1: Does your father usually find time to play with you?

Q2 What excuses does your father make when he doesn't play with you?

Q3: What about your mom? Is she usually ready to play with you? If not, what's her excuse?

5\. 

Q1: Do your parents nag you to get more exercise?

Q2 Do you think you should exercise more? Why or why not?

Q3: What are the excuses used by people who do not exercise enough?

6\. Q1: Do you enjoy video games? Why or why not?

Q2 How much time spent on video games is too much? Are you addicted to them?

Q3: What do your parents think about video games? Do you agree with their opinion?

LESSON 16 No Buts!

Answer Me

1 It Slipped My Mind

Mom : Oh, Ronnie. I'm sorry. I forgot all about your birthday. But I'll make it up to you.

Ron : How could you forget?

Mom : Actually, I didn't really forget when your birthday was. I know the date! But I just didn't realize it was today, until it was too late to do anything about it. I hope you can forgive me.

Ron : It's OK. Sometimes people forget things.

Mom : What have you forgotten?

Ron : Oops! I have a big project due. I have to get to work on it right away.

Mom : I'll help you with it.

Ron : It's a good thing that I'm not having a birthday party today. Otherwise, I'd never finish my homework!

Mom : Don't worry. Tomorrow we'll celebrate its completion and your birthday too!

Responsibility before pleasure!

Questions

1. Do your parents always remember your birthday?
2. If they forgot it, what would you do?
3. Do you always remember your parents' birthdays? When are they?

2 A Shift in Priorities

Mom : Why don't you help me with household chores?

Simon : I want to, but I have a lot of homework to do.

Mom : Do you have a lot of homework every night?

Simon : Yes. I have way too much to do. I can't help it.

Mom : OK, I guess I'll have to do everything all by myself every night. But that means I won't have any time to fix supper. I hope you can get by on just two meals a day, or prepare your own.

Simon : Um, what would you like some help with?

I hate to cook! Maybe I should have helped Mom sooner.

Questions

1. Do you help your parents with household chores? Why or why not?
2. What do you do to help? Name specific chores you help with.
3. Do you get extra pocket money for helping out?

LESSON 16 No Buts!

Answer Me

3 Little Confusion Grows Worse

Dad : Why don't you study harder?

Catherine : I want to, but I don't always understand the assignment. My teacher isn't very clear.

Dad : Why don't you ask him to explain it?

Catherine : Well, I'm afraid I'd look foolish. Everyone else seems to understand what to do. I don't want them to make fun of me.

Dad : But when you turn in your homework and it's not done right, don't you feel stupid then?

Catherine : Well, yes, of course.

Dad : You could avoid that, and get better grades too, if you made sure the assignment was clear before you got started on it.

Catherine : Yes, I suppose so.

Questions

1. Do you think you study hard enough? If not, why not?
2. What do your parents think about your grades? Are they happy?
3. Do you think studying is easy or hard? Why?

4 An Early Start

Linda : Hi, Ian.

Ian : Hello, Linda. Do you want to play with me?

Linda : Sure. But I can't right now.

Ian : Why not?

Linda : I have to study for a big test. Don't you?

Ian : Yes, but that's not for another two weeks. You don't need to study for it so soon.

Linda : Yes I do. I usually wait until the last minute, and then I don't do very well. So, this time I'm going to get an early start and make sure I know everything.

Ian : Maybe you're right. I guess I'll get started too.

Linda : Do you want to study together?

Ian : Sure.

Getting started earlier is a lot easier than cramming at the last moment.

Questions

1. How often do you play with your friends? What games do you usually play?
2. What do you say when you don't want to play with your friends?
3. Do you prepare for your tests every day or do you always cram for them?

LESSON 16 No Buts!

Let's Talk More

1 Honesty Is The Best Policy

I want my friends to be frank with me in all situations. That's why I ask their advice. If they tell me I look good in a new pair of jeans, but in fact they think I look terrible in them, they should tell me before I buy them! I can appreciate that my friends don't want to hurt my feelings, but they would be better friends if they were completely honest with me.

Questions

1. Do you really want your friends to be frank with you? What if they told you bad things about yourself?
2. Can you be perfectly frank with your friends? Why or why not?
3. When do you usually not tell your friends the complete truth?

2 Who Is Busy Now?

When somebody says "I'm busy" it really means "I'm lazy." We all have 24 hours in a day. Even when we deduct the time we need to sleep, we still have a lot of time to do whatever we want. If necessary, we can even eat while we do it. A wise man (my father) once told me, "When you need something done, go to the busiest person." That's because busy people always find a way to budget their time to make sure it gets done, but lazy people just make excuses.

Questions

1. Do you agree that "too-busy" people are really just being lazy? Explain your answer.
2. Do you believe your friend when he says "I'm sorry, I'm busy"?
3. What other excuses do people use instead of just saying, "I'm busy."?

LESSON 16 No Buts!

Let's Talk More

• 3 Busy Taking Naps

Adults are supposed to set a good example. They teach us by what they do, not by what they say. So if they tell me they're busy, but all they're doing is watching television or taking a nap, it's very difficult for me to believe them. But if I saw them working at something, I would already know that they're busy and wouldn't need to ask them to help me. Why do you think we're too stupid to notice things like this?

• Questions

1. Do you think most kids know when adults are just making excuses?
2. What are the most common excuses adults make to children? To other adults?
3. What are the most common excuses kids make to each other? To adults?

4 More Than One Truth?

OK, I'll tell you the truth. The reason I couldn't meet you last night was that I had a date with another person. I could have lied and said that I was sick, but I want to have an honest relationship with you. I really do want to keep seeing you, though, so I don't understand why you want to break off our relationship. Can't you handle the truth?

Questions

1. What would happen if everybody told the truth all the time?
2. "Telling the truth is always better than making excuses." Do you agree? Why or why not?
3. What positive consequences does lying sometimes have? Are there any?

LESSON 16 No Buts!

Real Talk

Needlessly Worried?

Mom : Peter?

Peter : Yes, Mom.

Mom : I'm very worried about your behavior these days.

Peter : What's wrong?

Mom : Don't you ever read anything but comic books?

Peter : You know I have to read a lot of books for school. But, in my own spare time, I like to read these. I think they're very interesting and relaxing.

Mom : But you just lie around the house all day, reading comic books and playing video games. Why don't you get more exercise?

Peter : Because I don't need to. I'm healthy, and I probably don't weigh enough as it is.

Mom : And you watch too much TV!

Peter : But watching TV is fun. And I learn a lot that way!

Mom : But I think you need to study more.

Peter : My grades are good, and the tests are still many weeks off. If I study for them now, I'll just have to do it all over again when testing time comes.

Mom : And you don't spend any time with your family.

Peter : I'm sorry. Why don't we all go see a movie?

Questions

1. At first, what behavior is Peter's mother concerned about?
2. What is Peter's excuse?
3. What else is she concerned about?
4. What is his excuse for that?

Read Me

Different Degrees of Untruth

Is there any difference between an excuse and a lie? I suppose it depends on the circumstances. A lie is something that is not true. More than that, it is a deliberate falsehood. Sometimes people can say untrue things, because they wrongfully think they are true. Excuses may be absolutely true, because sometimes events get out of control. Many times, though, excuses are only partially true. If I say that I didn't do my homework because I got home late, that may not be a lie: Maybe I did get home later than usual, but I still had enough time to do my homework — I just lacked the desire to do it; I COULD have done it, despite the lateness of the hour. There is an odd kind of excuse called a "rationalization." Basically, this amounts to a person lying to himself to provide a convenient reason for not doing something, but it is a very flimsy excuse indeed; no one else is fooled by it, only the person who says it.

One person's lie is another's excuse.
I guess it is a matter of perspective.

Questions

1. Do you think there is a difference between an excuse and a lie? If so, what is it?
2. In your own words, describe what a rationalization is. Give an example.
3. Do you feel guilty when you lie or make excuses? Why or why not?

Chat Room for Teens 02

LESSON 17 Is TV Really a Boob Tube?

Warm-up Dialog

The Value of Television

Dad : I'm going to turn off the TV. You watch too much television.

Carol : No, Dad! Please!

Dad : All you've done since you came home is sit here in front of the boob tube.

Carol : It helps me study. If the room is too quiet I can't concentrate.

Dad : I find that hard to believe. What I think is that it just makes you a passive observer without any imagination of your own or any involvement in the world.

Carol : No, actually I learn a lot from TV. Just think how much of the world I've seen on television. Reading about something is one thing, but actually seeing it is something else altogether.

Dad : But I don't think the soap operas and music programs you watch all the time show you very much of the world, do they?

Carol : You'd be surprised! I really learn a lot about how people behave toward one another. But that's not all I watch, you know.

Dad : I don't see you watching very much educational television. All you see are entertainment shows.

Carol : But, Dad, you don't understand. If I didn't watch those shows sometimes, I wouldn't have any friends left.

Dad : What are you talking about? If you weren't in front of the TV screen all the time, you'd be able to spend more time with your friends.

Carol : But then we wouldn't have anything to talk about! Most of our conversations are about what's on TV. Nobody would want to be with me if I couldn't talk about our favorite subject.

• Questions

1. Why does Carol's dad want to turn off the television?
2. Give three reasons why Carol wants to watch TV.
3. Can all of her reasons be true? Explain your answer.

Pictures

1. 

Q1: How many hours do you watch television every day? What do you watch?

Q2 Do you often watch TV late at night? Why or why not?

Q3: What do your parents think about your watching TV, especially late at night?

2. Q1: Do you eat snacks when you watch TV? Why or why not? What do you usually eat, if anything?

Q2 What might happen if you eat too much when watching TV?

Q3: Are there any healthy snacks? Name a few, in your opinion.

3. 

Q1: Do you ever argue with your brother or sister about which program to watch?

Q2 How do you usually solve the problem?

Q3: If you want to watch one show but your parents want a different one, what happens? What do you do?

Talk

4. Q1: Do you ever watch adult programs? Why or why not?

Q2 What do your parents think about your watching adult programs?

Q3: Why are some kinds of programs considered not appropriate for kids to watch? Do you agree?

5.

Q1: Does your family often watch TV together? Why or why not?

Q2 What do you talk about while watching TV? Or do you avoid talking at all?

Q3: Some people say watching TV interferes with family conversation. Do you agree? Give examples to support your view.

6. Q1: Which do you use more frequently, a TV or a computer?

Q2 It is said that kids watch less TV than their parents because the computer can do everything the TV does, thanks to the internet. Do you agree? Give your reasons.

Q3: If that is true, why do kids still watch TV?

LESSON 17 Is TV Really a Boob Tube?

Answer Me

1 At Home with the Electronic Babysitter

Brian : Hi.

Brenda : Hi, Brian. What are you doing?

Brian : Just watching television.

Brenda : I didn't think anything interesting is on this time of day.

Brian : Oh, it's not very interesting. It's just on, that's all.

Brenda : If it isn't interesting, why don't you do something else?

Brian : Nobody else is home, so I'm bored. TV takes my mind off being lonely.

Brenda : Where are your parents?

Brian : They both work. They should be home in a few hours.

Brenda : Aren't you scared, being home by yourself?

Brian : No..... Well, sometimes.

Brenda : Why don't you meet me in the park? I'm not busy, and we can have some fun together.

Brian : No, I'm not allowed to. I have to stay home till they get here.

Questions

1. Do you usually watch TV when you are home alone? If so, what kind of program do you watch?
2. Do your parents know you watch TV when you are alone? What do they say about it?
3. What else do you do when you are alone?

• 2 My Uncle TV?

Bonnie : Sometimes I don't understand my parents at all.

Gene : I know what you mean. I can't figure mine out, either.

Bonnie : They call our television an "idiot box."

Gene : Mine call ours a "boob tube."

Bonnie : And yet, my dad gets golf lessons on TV, and Mom is learning how to cook French food that way.

Gene : Both of mine watch the news and the opera on TV. They'd never be able to get out to see a live opera.

Bonnie : And I study many subjects that way myself, including English.

Gene : It's a treasure chest, not an idiot box!

Bonnie : I think it's more like part of the family. A wise, funny uncle who never gets tired of keeping me company.

• Questions

1. Do you learn things from TV? If so, what? If not, why not?
2. Do your parents ever study anything on TV, or do they think watching television is just a leisure pastime?
3. What do you think is the most useful function that TV has?

LESSON 17 Is TV Really a Boob Tube?

Answer Me

• 3 No More Television

Denise : Did you watch that new show last night? It was wonderful!

Ronnie : No, I can't. We don't have a TV anymore.

Denise : What! Isn't it boring?

Ronnie : Last month, my parents decided that we were all wasting too much time in front of the set. So they gave it away.

Denise : What a terrible thing to do! I feel sorry for you.

Ronnie : I felt pretty sorry for myself at first. But then I got used to it. Actually, not having a TV isn't so bad.

Denise : How do you spend your free time?

Ronnie : Well, I read more. I even read the newspaper now! And I go outside a lot more, so I'm in better shape. And I used to neglect my coin collecting hobby, but I've gotten interested in that again. Not having a television is the best thing that's happened to us recently.

Denise : But don't you miss your favorite shows and the football games?

Ronnie : Sometimes. But not as much as I thought I would.

No longer a slave to TV!
Now I'm free to read and think on my own.

• Questions

1. Why don't you try to persuade your parents to get rid of your family TV? Do you think they would do so? Why or why not?
2. What would be the worst thing that would happen if your family didn't have a TV anymore?
3. Who watches the most TV at your home?

4 Two Views of News

Gloria : Why are you reading the newspaper? Why not just get the news on TV?

Dad : Well, you know, sometimes I watch TV news too. But the two kinds are very different.

Gloria : How?

Dad : News on TV is good when it's covering something that is happening live. It's a lot like actually being there while it happens. That's an experience you can't get with a newspaper.

Gloria : Then why read about it?

Dad : Not everything happens in front of a television camera, you know.

Gloria : I guess you're right.

Dad : And the news on TV usually doesn't go very deep into the subject. A very brief account is given, and it's all over in a few seconds.

Gloria : That's true.

Dad : But newspapers usually have more analysis, so I can understand the issues better. And I can take my time reading it. If there's something that isn't clear, I can go back and read it again.

Gloria : Yes, you can't do that with the television news!

Questions

1. Do you pay attention to the news at all? Why or why not?
2. What advantages does television have?
3. What are the advantages of reading a newspaper or news magazine?

LESSON 17 Is TV Really a Boob Tube?

—— Let's Talk More ——

• 1 Bigotry Against TV

Too many parents are prejudiced against TV. They regard watching television as nothing but an obstacle to study. But they won't get rid of it, because they too enjoy watching it. It's another example of parents saying one thing while doing something else. On the other hand, a lot of kids think of television as a source of good topics to talk about, news about their favorite entertainers, and what the latest fashion trends are. So, for them, television has a great deal of social value.

What are you doing?
I thought you told me watching TV was bad.

• Questions

1. What do your parents think about TV?
2. Do you get useful information from watching TV? Can you give us some recent examples?
3. Do you ever feel isolated if you don't know what TV shows your friends are talking about?

• 2 Hooked or Not?

"TV addict." That is what Mom calls me. I admit that I watch TV two or three hours a day, but that doesn't make me an addict. I can still concentrate on my homework, and I usually finish my studying before I turn the TV on. And I think it is strange that she never calls herself a TV addict, even though she watches more than I do.

• Questions

1. How much time do your parents spend watching TV? Is this more or less time than you watch TV?
2. How would you describe a TV addict? Do you think that you are one? Why or why not?
3. If you or anyone in your family is a TV addict, what can be done about it?

Let's Talk More

3 Becoming Ourselves

I just discovered something, by accident. I suddenly realized that about 80% of the way my friends talk, dress, and think is a direct copy of what they see on TV. It's amazing, now that I put it in perspective. I can just "see" my best friend trying to look and sound like a TV character, even using the same words and hand gestures to make a point. I don't even think that he is aware of it himself. I wonder if I do the same thing.

Questions

1. Do you and your friends copy what you see on TV? Can you think of some examples of this?
2. Which TV celebrities are the most copied, in your opinion?
3. Do you think adults do it too?

• 4 The Best Part of Television

I often think the commercials are more interesting than the actual programs on TV. A great deal of money and planning is devoted to making TV ads, because of the very limited time available to make their point. The ad has to make an intense impression immediately. The look, the script, the actors, the music, and the message all have to be done just right, or the commercial will not work well. That is why many contemporary directors get their start making commercials, and that is also why the pace of modern movies is so much faster than it used to be.

• Questions

1. Are commercials really the most interesting programs on television? Explain your answer.
2. What is your favorite commercial?
3. Do commercials cause you to buy the advertised product? Are you sure?

LESSON 17 Is TV Really a Boob Tube?

Real Talk

What If There Were Five Family Members?

Harry : Mom, can I watch a comedy on a different channel? My friends say it's really funny.

Mom : I'm sorry, but you know my favorite soap opera is on right now. I don't want to miss any of it. You can watch your show after mine is over.

Harry : But it won't be over then! It's only a half hour long.

Mom : Hush! I want to watch this. Why don't you do your homework until I'm finished?

Harry : I never get to do what I want!

Mom : That's not true. Your dad and I have both given up a lot of things we wanted, just so you could be happy. But this time, I'm going to watch my favorite show, and then you can watch whatever you want after that. Meanwhile, I want you to be quiet.

Harry : It's not fair!

Mom : Look, your father and I paid for this TV, not you! You're not the boss in this household, you know.

Dad : I got home just in time. The big soccer match is on TV, and I don't want to miss it.

Mom : But I want to watch my soap opera. You know I never miss it.

Harry : I want to see the new comedy. All my friends watch it.

Dad : You know I hardly ever care what's on TV, but this game is important. I bet a lot of money on it, and I want to see it.

Mom : Will both of you be quiet!

Harry : Maybe we need two more TV sets, so we can each watch what we want to.

If we didn't argue about channel selection, we probably wouldn't talk at all.

Questions

1. Why does Harry want to go to a different channel?
2. When his father gets home, what does he want to see? Why?
3. Can they resolve the problem in a satisfactory manner? How could they prevent this problem in the future?

Read Me

What You See Is Not Always the Whole Truth

TV can give us many wrong impressions. The most dramatic scenes are the ones that are aired, not the ordinary, more genuine, ones. For example, if there is a bad typhoon in the south, my friends at home in the United States always call me or email me asking if I'm all right. Or if there is a violent demonstration, they are concerned, even if it has happened miles away from where I am. Because the TV is in our living room, we think that it must be showing us what is real, but the bigger picture is simply not revealed to us. I wonder what conditions are actually like in Nigeria or North Korea, and how those conditions are different than what I see on TV.

There's a lot of world beyond the TV camera lens.

Questions

1. Does television give us the complete picture of what is happening? Can it? Explain your answer.
2. What are the most misleading aspects of what we watch on TV?
3. How can we find out about what the television cameras miss?

Chat Room for Teens 02

LESSON 18 I Want to Invent a "Studying Machine"

Warm-up Dialog

Taking Things For Granted

Mom : Oops.

Harry : Mom! What happened?

Mom : Don't worry. The power just went off. I'm sure it will come back on soon.

Harry : But I was in the middle of my favorite game!

Mom : And my favorite TV show just came on. But there's nothing we can do about it except wait.

Harry : What are we going to do now? We don't even have any lights!

Mom : Yes, it makes you think, doesn't it? How did people live before they had electricity?

A simple outage or a complete blackout—either way, we can do nothing.

Harry : You're right, Mom. No computers, no stereo, no TV or DVD. What did they do?

Mom : Even more seriously, without refrigerators, they couldn't keep their food from spoiling.

Harry : And without elevators, we'd have to walk all the way up to our apartment. That would be hard!

Mom : Just think about all the inventions we take for granted. We don't even think about them except when we can't use them for some reason, but we really can't do without them.

Harry : Like cars and phones?

Mom : Right.

Harry : I sure hope the electricity comes back soon. I've already lived that way for five minutes and wouldn't want to do so for a long period of time.

Questions

1. Describe the situation in your own words.
2. What would happen if we did not have electricity anymore?
3. What did people do before electrical devices became common?

Pictures

1.

Q1: What would happen if we had no refrigerators?

Q2 What would happen if we had no air conditioners?

Q3: What would happen if we had no microwave ovens?

2.

Q1: What would happen if we had no alarm clocks?

Q2 What would happen if we had no cars?

Q3: What would happen if we had no mobile phones?

3.

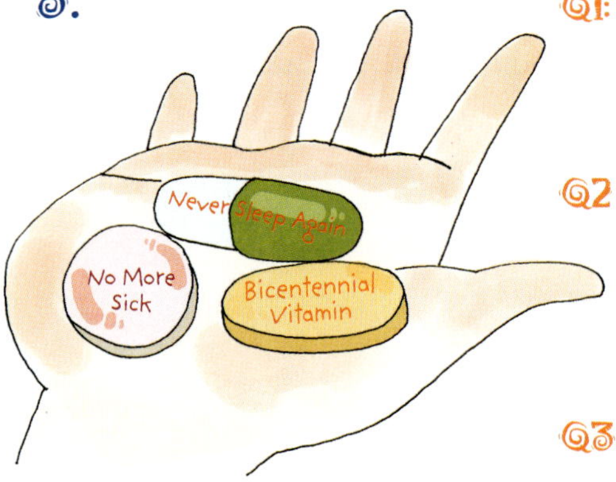

Q1: A panacea would treat all of our illnesses. Would you want to have one? Why or why not?

Q2 Would you want to have a tablet that could let you live for another century? Do you want to live forever? Why or why not?

Q3: If you could go forever without sleeping, would you want such a tablet?

Talk

4. Q1: Do you think a time machine is possible?

Q2 What would you want to do if you had one?

Q3: Do you want to know the future? Do you think we would be happier if we knew what was going to happen in advance?

5.

Q1: Could you exist without the Internet? What did people do before it was invented?

Q2 List a couple of major services Internet provides.

Q3: Can you imagine the Internet after 10 years?

6. Q1: Do you have any good ideas for an invention? Describe its purpose.

Q2 Do you think people can invent absolutely anything they want?

Q3: Do you think men can achieve happiness through their imagination alone? Why or why not?

LESSON 18 I Want to Invent a "Studying Machine"

—— Answer Me ——

• 1 The Cook's Meal

Mom : I hate to cook! It's hard work, and I have to do it all over again every day.

Stuart : But you're a great cook! I always like everything you fix.

Mom : I wish someone would invent a tablet that we only had to take once a month — or, once a year! — that would give us all the nutrition we need. Then I wouldn't have to cook anymore.

Stuart : You mean we'd only eat once a year?

Mom : No, we'd just take a pill. We wouldn't ever have to eat at all.

Stuart : That's a terrible idea!

Mom : Why?

Stuart : Because I like to eat! Especially the dishes you make.

Mom : Well, you're lucky then, since nobody's invented such a thing yet. But why don't you help me cook? You can start by cutting up some vegetables for me.

• Questions

1. Would you approve of such a tablet? Why or why not?
2. Do you enjoy eating?
3. Do you eat three meals a day? What do you usually have for each one?

• 2 The Solution!

Dad : Ooooooh! I hate this traffic.

Vince : We've just stayed in the same place for a long time.

Dad : We're supposed to be out for a drive, not sitting in a "parking lot" for an hour.

Vince : I've got to go to the bathroom.

Dad : You're just going to have to wait until we can move again. There isn't any place around here.

Vince : Well, while we're waiting, why don't you invent a flying car? Then we could just go!

Dad : What a wonderful idea! But I'm sure others have already thought about that.

Vince : But nobody's done it yet!

Dad : Sikorsky, the inventor of the helicopter, thought every family would eventually have one. But that never happened.

Vince : Why not?

Dad : Oh, maybe the expense. And the danger. Can you imagine the whole sky filled with bad drivers, going in any and every direction at once?

Now bad drivers can come at me from any direction, even up and down.

• Questions

1. Do you want a flying car? Why or why not?
2. Do you think heavy traffic puts too much stress on drivers?
3. What are some practical solutions to traffic problems?

Answer Me

3 Hair Troubles

Wyatt : What's wrong, Mom? You look worried about something.

Mom : Oh, I found a gray hair in my comb this morning. I guess I'm getting old.

Wyatt : No, you're not!

Mom : Yes, I am. Soon, all my hair will turn gray and then white, and I'll need a cane or a walker to get around.

Wyatt : But you're still young and healthy.

Mom : I feel pretty good, but that gray hair...

Wyatt : Just dye it.

Mom : Dyes only last a little while. And they don't look natural. What I need is some sort of medicine that keeps my hair from changing color.

Wyatt : That would be a good idea. I bet the inventor of that would make a lot of money.

Mom : Why don't you invent it, then? We could use the money.

Wyatt : I have an even better idea!

Mom : What's that?

Wyatt : An anti-balding medicine! I know how much Dad suffers from losing his hair. I think going bald is even worse than getting gray.

Questions

1. Do either of your parents suffer from gray hair or baldness? What is their attitude about it?
2. Are you worried about becoming bald or having gray hair someday?
3. How much money do you think the person who invents an anti-balding medicine could make?

4 A New Weather Channel

Ivan : I want to go outside and play!

Priscilla : Me, too! But it rains every day!

Ivan : We need more sunshine.

Priscilla : My parents say the farmers need the rain.

Ivan : They've had plenty of water for the last week. Now it's my turn! I want a nice sunny day so I can play.

Priscilla : OK. I'll make a weather machine.

Ivan : A what?

Priscilla : A weather machine. We could select our weather, just like we choose the TV channel we want to watch or a music file on our iPod.

Ivan : You're a genius.

Priscilla : Well, I haven't worked out all the details yet. But it is a good idea, isn't it?

Do I want it to snow first and then get hot, or the other way around?

Questions

1. Do you like sunny days or rainy weather better? Why?
2. Do you feel blue when it's rainy?
3. Would we be happy if we could change the weather whenever we wanted? Why or why not?

LESSON 18 I Want to Invent a "Studying Machine"

Let's Talk More

1 Time to End This Evil Practice!

I like to eat fish, fried chicken, hamburgers, and grilled pork. I eat meat every day and can't imagine becoming a vegetarian. But every time I go into a fast food restaurant or eat a good meal at home, I feel guilty. What gives us the right to kill other living beings just so we can eat them? They have the same right to live as I do! Actually, the same is true for plants, too. Why do we have to kill in order to survive? Why can't we just eat healthy chemical food that tastes good and is nutritious? That way the murder of innocent plants and animals could stop.

Questions

1. Do you like meat? What about vegetables? What are your least favorite foods?
2. Do you ever think about the animals that are killed for your diet?
3. Would you be willing to eat artificial meat if that prevented the killing of other creatures?

2 Even Better Than an Electric Dog

I need a better friend! My human friends are unreliable. They aren't always around when I need them, or they don't completely understand what I need. Sometimes we fight together. So I want a robot friend which I could program to meet my every need. It could comfort me when I'm sad, play with me when I'm lonely, and help me with my homework.

Questions

1. Do you like the idea of having a robot friend?
2. What would be the good points and bad points of that?
3. What kinds of robots do you think would be the most useful?

LESSON 18 I Want to Invent a "Studying Machine"

Let's Talk More

• 3 Is It a Good Idea?

I could solve most of my problems if I knew what other people were thinking. Then I would know who my real friends were, and what my teachers really thought about me. I wouldn't get into as much trouble with my parents. In sports, I could anticipate every move my opponents made. I wouldn't have to study hard for tests, since I could easily read somebody else's answer. What a wonderful invention a mind-reading gadget would be!

• Questions

1. What would the advantages and disadvantages be of reading your friends' minds?
2. Do you want to read your teachers' mind? Why or why not?
3. Would you want everyone else to be able to read your mind? Why or why not?

• 4 Always Be Careful What You Wish For — It Could Come True

The greatest invention in the world would be a Destiny Machine. I could program it at an early age and plot out my entire life. I could decide in advance who I would marry and what my kids would be like. I could plan on how rich I would be and where I would live. I could pre-determine how famous I would become and for what reasons. Health and a long life would be mine for the asking. Wouldn't that be wonderful?

Don't touch the DELETE key!
If I touched it, what would happen?

• Questions

1. What kind of life do you want? What are the most important aspects of life?
2. A Destiny Machine must be very expensive, don't you think? So probably only the super rich could afford one. Do you think that's fair?
3. What undesirable side effects do you think such a device could be responsible for?

LESSON 18 I Want to Invent a "Studying Machine"

Real Talk

No More School!

Sarah : How did you do on your test?

Randy : Not too good. And I thought I studied hard, too!

Sarah : I guess not hard enough. Maybe you need to spend less time goofing off with your friends.

Randy : I've got a better idea!

Sarah : What's that?

Randy : I'll invent a study machine!

Sarah : A what?

Randy : A study machine! Just plug it into our brains and we'll automatically know whatever we need. That way we don't have to waste all that time studying useless information and getting bad test grades.

Sarah : You're such a comedian!

Randy : What's so funny? I think it's a great idea!

Sarah : It's a stupid idea. It's impossible.

Randy : Well, you know, a hundred years ago space travel was impossible too. But we've landed on the moon and sent probes out beyond our solar system.

Sarah : Yes, but those things took many years and thousands of people to accomplish. I don't think you're going to invent a study machine all by yourself. Not with your bad grades!

Randy : Oh, yeah! You'll see. When I'm rich and famous, don't forget to remind me of all the help you've given.

• Questions

1. Do you want someone to invent a studying machine soon? Why or why not?
2. What would happen if everybody had such a machine?
3. Do you really think such a machine can actually be invented? Why?

Read Me

Unintended Consequences

Every great leap for mankind may lead to small steps backward for individuals. Just consider for a moment the unintended side-effects of some of the greatest inventions in history. The automobile has been a wonderful tool for moving us around cheaply, quickly, and conveniently. But for most of us, it means we no longer get enough exercise, and we have to breathe bad air (which is slowly killing us). The air conditioner has allowed us to move into some of the hottest places on the planet, but we can't endure hot weather anymore and we just stay inside all summer instead of being outdoors. Think about the humble clock: because of that simple device, our lives have become busier, and we have become slaves to time. All of the so-called "labor-saving" devices, from computers to household appliances, have just enabled us to do more work but have not given us any additional time to read, paint, write poetry, or contemplate the important things in life.

Anything gained means something is lost!

Questions

1. What are some negative consequences of atomic energy?
2. How have cell phones caused additional problems in our lives?
3. What have computers taken away from us?

Chat Room for Teens 02

LESSON 19 Habits Make Me

Warm-up Dialog

Easier Said Than Done?

Paula	:	Ms. Roberts, may I talk to you for a few minutes?
Ms. Roberts	:	Of course! What's up?
Paula	:	Oh, I don't know. I'm just very confused, I guess.
Ms. Roberts	:	What about?
Paula	:	Oh, just growing up. Things don't seem to be as clear as they used to be. My feelings about life are in a swirl. But I want to grow up to be a responsible adult. Can you help me?
Ms. Roberts	:	It's hard for girls your age — and boys, too, of course. I went through it myself. Your body is changing in all kinds of ways. The hormone balance is adjusting. Voices change, looks change. Kids are becoming adults, but they are still kids in many ways. It can be very strange.
Paula	:	But what can I do?
Ms. Roberts	:	A lot of life is just routine. We put one step in front of the other, then repeat and repeat and repeat. But it's important to be consistently walking in the right direction, or we'll just go around in circles.
Paula	:	Going in circles! That's the way I feel these days.
Ms. Roberts	:	Of course. But you just need to develop goods habits. Decide what you want to do, no matter how important or trivial it seems. And then think about how to get there, and consciously work toward that goal. Before you know it, you won't even think about it anymore, but you'll still be going in the right direction. Just like being on auto-pilot.
Paula	:	Can you be more specific? What do you mean?
Ms. Roberts	:	OK. Let's say you want to get more exercise. But, somehow, something always happens to interfere with your program.

No matter how hard it seems at the time, continuing on the right track is the only way to get where you're going.

Paula : How did you know?

Ms. Roberts : Like I said, I've gone through it.

Paula : So, what did you do?

Ms. Roberts : I made myself a schedule. As soon as I got home from school, I immediately changed clothes and took a walk. I made sure that I kept it up for at least a half hour. No matter what, I kept to my schedule. If a friend called, I'd say I'd call her back later. If it was raining, I'd take an umbrella. I was very single-minded about it. But, in about a month, it was second nature to me. Then, if I had to miss my walk for some reason, I really felt like I was in withdrawal. I've done that for 15 years now, hardly ever missing a day. It's become a habitual part of my life.

Paula : Wow. It sounds so easy.

Ms. Roberts : It wasn't always easy. But I kept at it. And it was only hard for a very short time, and then it just became natural. You can reach any goal that way.

Paula : That's very inspirational.

Ms. Roberts : The other side of the coin is that bad habits keep you from achieving your goals.

Paula : Yes, I certainly have a lot of those.

Ms. Roberts : So you need to deprogram those habits. Just beware of doing the things you don't want to do, and substitute something else. If you smoke and want to quit, chew some gum every time you reach for a pack of cigarettes. Instead of candy, eat an apple. Just be consistent, and you'll be all right.

Questions

1. Is our life ruled by habit?
2. What's the secret to building good exercise habits?
3. Apply the "habit method" to some other goal, and describe it.

Pictures

1.

Q1: Do you get up early in the morning by yourself, or does someone need to wake you up?

Q2 Who gets you up? Is it easy or hard to get you out of bed?

Q3: What time do you usually go to bed? When do you get up?

2.

Q1: Do you brush your teeth immediately after every meal?

Q2 Do you brush your teeth before you go to bed?

Q3: Do you take your toothbrush to school?

3.

Q1: How often do you wash your hands?

Q2 Why is washing one's hands so important?

Q3: Describe in detail how you wash your hands.

Talk

4. Q1: Do you keep a diary? Why or why not?

Q2 Is it easy to keep one? What are some of the problems involved in doing so?

Q3: What do you write about?

5.

Q1: Do you eat between meals? What do you eat?

Q2 Why do people snack?

Q3: What are some of the bad results of eating snacks?

6. Q1: Do you always say "Thanks"? Why or why not?

Q2 Do you always say "I'm sorry" when you think you are wrong?

Q3: Do you always say "I made a mistake"? Do you always mean it when you say it?

LESSON 19 Habits Make Me

Answer Me

• 1 Making Sure First

Derrick : Are you going to watch my team play basketball this weekend? It's the biggest game of the year.

Matilda : I hope so. But I have to ask my mom.

Derrick : It's during the daytime. So you won't be out late.

Matilda : I know. And I really want to go. But I still need permission.

Derrick : Why? You're not a child. You're old enough to make up your own mind.

Matilda : I do make my own decisions! But I still have to make sure it's OK. Maybe my family is going somewhere, and I might have to go too.

Derrick : But you're my girlfriend. It's important to me that you come watch me play. That way, I'll compete better.

Matilda : I'm sure it will be all right. But I can't say for sure right now.

• Questions

1. Do you always ask your parents for permission to do things?
2. What are you able to decide on your own?
3. If you do not agree with your parents' decision, what do you do?

• 2 Saving the Best for Last

Rod : Beth, I sure do envy you.

Beth : Why?

Rod : Because you're always ahead of everybody else in school. You always get the best grades and you never have to struggle to keep up. I have trouble just getting by!

Beth : Don't be too hard on yourself. You're a smart boy.

Rod : Then why is schoolwork so hard for me?

Beth : Because you always wait until the last minute to get started, and then you have to hurry, and you don't spend as much time on it as you should.

Rod : But I don't like to do homework! I hate to study!

Beth : Me, too. But that's why I do it right away. I always do the things I dislike first. That way I make sure they get done right, so I don't have to do them again. And, once I'm finished with them, I can spend the rest of the time enjoying myself, because I don't have to worry about them anymore.

Putting the unpleasant things behind oneself makes for a happy future.

• Questions

1. Are you satisfied with your grades?
2. If dissatisfied, what could you do to improve them?
3. What do you think about Beth's philosophy about doing first the things she dislikes the most?

Answer Me

3 To Eat? Or to Sleep? That is the Question

Mother : Dickie, you're getting fat. Your clothes don't fit right anymore.

Dickie : I know. But I don't know what to do about it. I get plenty of exercise.

Mother : I think it's those late-night snacks. You shouldn't eat just before you go to bed. All of those calories just turn to fat.

Dickie : But by bedtime I'm hungry. If I don't eat something then, I can't sleep.

Mother : At least you could eat something healthy, like an apple.

Dickie : OK, I'll try. But I sure do like ice cream!

The later it is, the better the snack!

Questions

1. Do you like to eat late at night? Why or why not?
2. If you eat late, what do you prefer to have?
3. What do your parents think about your eating at bedtime? Have they ever said why?

• 4 Free Without a Cellphone

Marie : I tried calling you all weekend. Where were you?

Mark : I went camping with my friends.

Marie : Why didn't you answer your phone?

Mark : Because I didn't take it with me.

Marie : Why not? Were you trying to avoid me?

Mark : Of course not. But sometimes I want to be left alone. That way I can reflect on life and what I should do, without anybody bothering me on the phone.

Marie : I can't imagine not having my phone with me. I need to talk to my friends.

Mark : Me, too. Most of the time. But sometimes I just feel like I'm a slave to my cellphone. If I leave it home, I feel free!

Kicking my phone habit would give me some private time.

• Questions

1. Do you sometimes have time alone? Why or why not?
2. About what do you think when you are all by yourself?
3. What's the most important thing on your mind these days?

Let's Talk More

• 1 How to Succeed

All too many times, we are our own worst enemies. We make up our minds in advance that something is too hard, so we don't waste our energy trying to do the impossible. Then failure becomes a self-fulfilling prophecy. The better approach is to decide that it can be done after all, and then be willing to put in the hard work necessary to make it happen. Sometimes, for a variety of reasons, we will still fail — but we'll succeed a lot more often than if we give up in advance. If you're positive that you can't do something, you won't. But if you're sure you can, you just might!

• Questions

1. Do you think you can do anything you put your mind to?
2. What have you failed at in the past? What could you have done differently to accomplish it?
3. Do you believe that a positive attitude always leads to positive results? Or do you think that some things are truly impossible, no matter what you do about it?

• 2 Everybody Likes Praise

A good habit to get into is being liberal with your praise. If you tell everyone what a good job he is doing and that you appreciate all his hard work, or that you really like him a great deal because of the kind of person he is, he will want to keep your good opinion of him and work even harder to please you. He will also feel better about himself, and, just as importantly, he'll find it easier to tell other people how wonderful you are. Before long, your positive reputation will spread well beyond just the two of you.

You can catch more flies with sugar than with vinegar.

• Questions

1. Are you in the habit of praising your friends?
2. Do your parents praise you often enough? What do they do when they want you to know they are proud of you?
3. What about your teachers? If they said more good things about you, would your school performance improve?

Let's Talk More

3 Do You Have Time?

We aren't all born with money or status. We don't all have the same intelligence and skill. But everyone has one thing in common: time. Learn not to waste a minute of it. Idling away our lives is a form of self-poison. This doesn't mean that life is only hard work. Even time spent enjoying oneself is time well spent. But certainly we need to balance enjoyment with self-improvement and with accomplishing necessary things. Just sitting around all the time — daydreaming and thinking about what might have been — won't get you anywhere.

One man wastes much time in laziness while another busy man seems to add hours to a day.

Questions

1. Do you think you use your time effectively? Why or why not? How could you improve?
2. What is the biggest time waster in your life?
3. What skill takes a lot of time and effort for you to master? Is there anything you can do easily, without much effort?

• 4 Who's In Charge?

Be patient. Always be patient. Then, patiently, continue. If you lose your temper every time you are angry, you will always defeat yourself. But if you can count to ten inside your head before you respond, you will get control of your emotions. Then you can work the situation to your own advantage. Patience will always accomplish more than temper. People may tell you that it is healthy to express your emotions, and that suppressing your feelings is bad for your mental health. But you need to take that advice one step further. You certainly should express what you feel, but you need to learn how to do that in a positive way. Be patient. It is not easy to learn how to master your emotions; but life will be a lot harder if you are a slave to them.

Emotions either weigh us down or launch us up, depending on how we control them.

• Questions

1. Do you think you are patient? Give us some examples of your patience or impatience.
2. What about your parents? Are they patient in the way they relate to you? Give examples of why you think so or don't think so.
3. What about your friends? Who's the most patient? The least? How does that aspect of their personality make their lives easier or more difficult?

LESSON 19 Habits Make Me

Real Talk

Two Things at Once

Mom : Henry, put that book away and eat.

Henry : Aw, Mom, I have a lot of homework tonight. If I don't finish this book, I'll be in a lot of trouble.

Mom : Then you should have started reading that book sooner!

Henry : I know, but I couldn't. I just didn't have enough time.

Mom : I'm sure you'll get it done tonight. But for now I want you to put it down. You can pick it up again after you finish your meal.

Henry : But why? I can do two things at the same time.

Mom : Probably so. But you can't do two things well. Please put that book away.

Henry : But this way I can kill two birds with one stone.

Mom : The proverb is that you CAN'T kill two birds with one stone.

Henry : OK, OK. I'll stop reading. There! I hope you're satisfied. But I still don't understand why it's such a big deal. I'm not hurting anybody.

Mom : Not directly, maybe. But it's bad manners. We don't spend much time together, but we can at least pay attention to each other at mealtime. That's not too much to ask.

Henry : But once in a while, in an emergency, spending time together won't matter.

Mom : This isn't an emergency! Besides, lots of studies have shown that being busy while eating is a terrible habit. People who enjoy their meals with other people, who talk and relax, are far healthier — and much more productive — than people who concentrate on work while they eat. So, if you're really worried about not having enough time, you'll be better off taking a few minutes off during this meal, and then when you go back to work you'll be refreshed and energetic. Do you understand?

Henry : Yes, Mom.

But I wonder. Wouldn't he learn more if the food didn't distract his attention? And wouldn't he enjoy his meal better if he wasn't trying to study at the same time?

Questions

1. What is Henry's problem?
2. What is his mother's problem with Henry?
3. How does he justify his actions? How does she justify hers? Who do think is right?

Read Me

Do We Get Habits or Do Habits Get Us?

Old habits die hard. You may wonder why it is that bad habits form easily and refuse to go away, but good habits are hard to create and disappear easily. It is because we readily do the things that are enjoyable, and we are reluctant to do the unpleasant (but necessary) things. We would all rather eat ice cream than broccoli, because ice cream tastes better. But then it's easy for us to want to keep eating too much ice cream and to ignore the broccoli altogether. We'd rather watch a good television program, or play an exciting computer game, than read a difficult book, because it's always easier to be passive than to have to actively use our intellect or imagination. We never have to be forced to do what we want to do. Old habits never die — but they do fade away from disuse.

Bad habits are a sure path to destruction, but good ones lead to gold.

Questions

1. What bad habits do you want to do away with? Why?
2. What good habit would you like to develop?
3. Tell how to build good habits and get rid of bad ones.

LESSON 20 The Computer is My Friend

Warm-up Dialog

The Computer is the Biggest Difference in the Generation Gap

Mom : Will you put that thing away?

Philip : What thing? My computer?

Mom : Yes. It's like it's attached to your body. Do you always have it with you?

Philip : Almost. I don't know how I'd get through school without it.

Mom : That's why we got it for you. But I didn't think we were buying you a new body part.

Philip : It's almost like that. It's like my right arm. This computer is my best friend.

Mom : I'm afraid that you spend too much time on games and not enough on your studies.

Philip : Don't worry. I get my schoolwork done early now, so I have more time to play, that's all. My grades are better than they've ever been.

I'm here, and all my friends are somewhere else, but we're still together all the time.

Mom : And you don't exercise.

Philip : Now that I listen to my music on my computer, I enjoy exercising more, so I don't find excuses to avoid exercise like I used to.

Mom : And most of all, I don't think you socialize enough. The computer isn't a person, it's just a machine. But you spend all your time on it.

Philip : A lot of the time is spent chatting with my friends. We don't have to waste time getting together, since we can all get in touch with each other instantaneously. So we're all a lot closer now than we used to be. And I've made lots of new friends, all over the world! Besides, now I can communicate with Grandpa anytime at all, so I feel lots closer to my family.

Mom : Maybe I'm just old-fashioned, but I just can't believe that this is a good development in the long run.

Questions

1. What is Philip's mother worried about?
2. What is Philip's explanation?
3. What do you think about Mom's last statement? Do you agree?

Pictures

1.

Q1: Would a computer be helpful in studying or doing your homework? How?

Q2 A computer is said to be a "second teacher." Do you agree? Which one does a better job, the computer or a teacher?

Q3: Computers are said to be a "second parent." Do you agree? In what ways?

2.

Q1: How often do you enjoy online games? What kinds of games do you usually play?

Q2 How often do you chat online? What do you usually talk about? With whom?

Q3: Are your parents worried about your computer usage?

3.

Q1: How often do you surf the Internet?

Q2 What kinds of websites do you usually visit?

Q3: Do you check your email every day?

Talk

4\.

Q1: Do your parents shop online? Why or why not?

Q2 What have you bought online? Were you satisfied with the shopping experience?

Q3: People say online shopping makes us into shopaholics. Do you agree? Why?

5\.

Q1: Do you have a blog? If so, describe it. If not, what kind of blog would you like to have?

Q2 What are the good things and bad things about having one's own blog?

Q3: How much time does it take to maintain a good blog?

6\.

Q1: What club activities do you do online?

Q2 What are good and bad things about doing them online rather than in person?

Q3: How often do you meet other members face to face?

LESSON 20 The Computer is My Friend

Answer Me

1 More Memory!

Jeremy : I need a new computer.

Mom : Why? Is yours broken? We just got it a few months ago.

Jeremy : It's been over a year. And it won't play the new games I want to play.

Mom : Why not?

Jeremy : The memory isn't big enough. I need a new one.

Mom : Do you realize how much a new computer costs? We can't just get a new one every year, simply because newer ones are faster or hold more games!

Jeremy : But I need it for my homework too.

Mom : You don't have enough memory to do your school work? How many gigs of information do you need? Do you have to write a book every week?

Jeremy : Well, no.

Mom : We didn't get you a computer to have fun with. We got it to help you at school. That's all.

Jeremy : Well, if I've finished all my schoolwork, it's okay if I use it for other things too, isn't it?

Mom : Yes. But only AFTER you're done.

Jeremy : Then, can I at least get more memory?

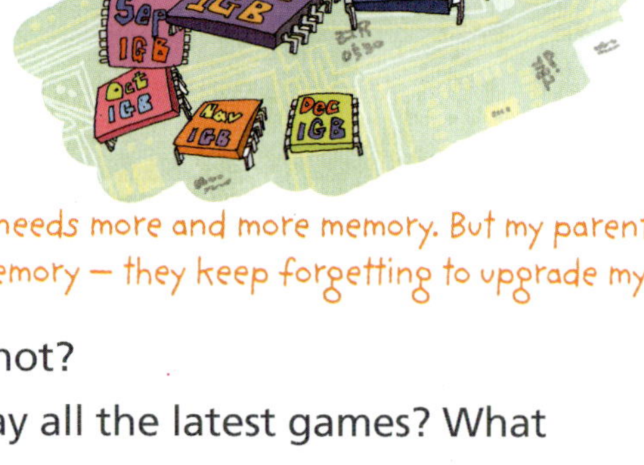

My computer needs more and more memory. But my parents are losing their memory – they keep forgetting to upgrade my PC.

Questions

1. Do you enjoy video games? Why or why not?
2. Is your computer advanced enough to play all the latest games? What would you like to play but can't?
3. How old is your computer? Do your parents always say "yes" whenever you ask for a new one?

I think Mom misunderstood me when
I asked her to get me some more Spam.

2 Today's Spam Eats You!

Harry : I hate that!

Janet : What?

Harry : All this spam! It takes up too much space on my drive, and it takes too long to go through it all to find out what's important.

Janet : I know it's frustrating. I don't like spam either. But you can eliminate many of the hassles.

Harry : How?

Janet : Well, first off, you should never open any email from an unfamiliar address. If you don't know who sent it, it's probably spam. And it might contain a dangerous virus.

Harry : I know that. But it still takes a lot of time scrolling through all my mail to identify the ones I don't know.

Janet : Haven't you used the screening services your server provides?

Harry : I guess not. What are they?

Janet : Well, why don't you take me to your computer, and I'll show you what I mean.

Harry : OK. Send me an email and we'll set up an appointment.

Janet : But you don't know my email address! Why would you open any message if you don't know who sent it?

Harry : Well, I like to make new friends.

Janet : But that's why you're plagued with so much spam!

Questions

1. What do you think about spam? Do you get angry about it, or doesn't it bother you much? Or, are you one of those people who enjoy spam?
2. Why do people send spam mail? In most cases, what is the sender trying to do?
3. Do you think spammers should be harshly punished by law? What would be an appropriate sentence?

LESSON 20 The Computer is My Friend

Answer Me

3 Reading Is Too Old-Fashioned

Dwight : Hi. Are you listening to a new CD?

Darlene : Well, yes, but it's not what you think.

Dwight : You mean it isn't rap?

Darlene : Oh, it's rap all right. But it isn't rap music!

Dwight : I'm confused. What do you mean?

Darlene : I'm listening to someone read a book!

Dwight : Why would you do that? Why don't you just read a book on your own?

Darlene : I do, all the time, of course. But sometimes it isn't convenient. Like on a crowded subway or in a car. I just can't concentrate very well then, but I can still listen.

Dwight : What kinds of ebooks do you like?

Darlene : All kinds! It depends on my mood. But the educational ones are the ones that I listen to most often. I've learned a lot in recent months, especially about ancient history.

It's amazing. I can have the world's library with me wherever I go.

Questions

1. Have you ever "read" an ebook?
2. What are the advantages and disadvantages of ebooks and regular books?
3. Do you think paper books will disappear soon? Give your reasons.

• 4 Contagion

Keith : Did you finish your report?

Toni : Yes, of course. Yesterday! Didn't you?

Keith : No. I was almost done, but then my computer stopped working.

Toni : It's probably a virus.

Keith : Yes, that's what my dad thinks too. But it's going to take too long to fix it. I've got to finish my report tonight!

Toni : Would you like to use my computer? I'm done.

Keith : Can I? That sure would help a lot!

Toni : But I want you to be careful. I don't want to get your virus!

Keith : Don't worry! I'll be extremely cautious.

Toni : Then how did your computer get a virus in the first place, if you were so cautious?

The virus wars never end.

• Questions

1. How do computers get infected with viruses?
2. Why do some people make viruses and spread them?
3. In cyber germ warfare, which is more likely to win, the viruses or the vaccines?

Let's Talk More

1 X's And Q's

The X Generation finally seems to have grown up! Thank goodness! But maybe it has been replaced by the Q Generation. The Q stands for Quiet. Unlike the Xers, who were loud and obnoxious, the Q's enjoy being by themselves. They are not hermits; they have lots of friends. But they'd rather communicate with them privately, by email, than to go out and meet them in person. They say it is more convenient, safer, and more efficient than personal contact.

Questions

1. Are you a member of the Q generation?
2. Which do you like better, chatting on a computer or being with your friends live?
3. What are the advantages of chatting online? What are the disadvantages?

• 2 You Need More Words

Modern computer users are reinventing language. In order to save time, they are inventing a lot of new words and punctuation marks. The words tend to be abbreviations of longer words and phrases, while the punctuation marks are mostly used to provide emotional commentary. As their usage grows, a person who does not chat much online may find it harder and harder to maintain communication with the netizens, but nevertheless many of the expressions are finding their way into standard dictionaries.

ILIDOD (Internet language is destroying our dictionary)

• Questions

1. Are you able to use these online expressions easily without having to think about their meaning?
2. List some online acronyms which are commonly used. What expressions do they stand for?
3. Are you worried about the trend? Why or why not?

Let's Talk More

• 3 If Your Computer Has All the Memory, Where is Yours?

Nowadays, if people want to know about something, they can usually find it out by searching the Net. Now, no one has to remember anything, since they can get any information they need. They don't even have to go to a library anymore. But is that desirable? What if a massive power outage would erase all the information on the Internet? If nobody knew how to do things on their own, would mankind go back into the Stone Age?

Ask me anything! My search engines can find the answer.

• Questions

1. What kinds of information do you usually search for (such as academic subjects or hobbies or personal information)?
2. You don't have to remember everything, thanks to the "search engine"! And you don't have to study anymore, either, right? Why or why not?
3. What roles do teachers have in this internet era? Are they no longer necessary?

• 4 I Don't Like My First Life!

As you may know, some companies are starting to provide customers with a "second life" in cyber space, in which they can change themselves into any fictional version they wish. They can become beautiful models, rich CEOs, successful athletes, or brilliant scientists. In short, they may fulfill their wildest fantasies — but only in an imaginary, computer-generated world of their own creation. Is this just harmless daydreaming in an electronic age, or is it likely to become a serious problem as users become more and more detached from reality? Or, is it a way of projecting our hopes onto an external reality, as a means of actualizing them in the future?

I used to be rich and famous in my imagination only, but now in cyberspace I really am.

• Questions

1. If it were affordable, would you want to establish a "second life"? How about a third or fourth one?
2. Is this any different than having an avatar in a computer game? If so, how?
3. Reinvent yourself—what kind of "second life" would you like to have? Be specific.

LESSON 20 The Computer is My Friend

Real Talk

If the Computer Does All the Work, Would We Then Be the Slaves?

Rachel : I don't want to be a computer.

Mr. Jackson : Don't worry. You can't ever be one. You're a flesh-and-blood human being, not a bundle of wires and electrons.

Rachel : But I don't want to be replaced by a computer, either.

Mr. Jackson : What are you concerned about?

Rachel : Computers are doing almost everything that people used to do, except much faster and without making as many mistakes.

Mr. Jackson : Yes, that's true, especially for repetitive, time-consuming, manual labor. But they just do what they're programmed to do. They can't think for themselves. They're actually very stupid, but fast.

Rachel : But the artificial intelligence technology is developing so quickly, I'm afraid they will soon be able to think and even imagine anything on their own.

Mr. Jackson : Hmmmmm. Perhaps, someday. But I doubt if it will really happen. And if it ever does, it will be far in the future.

Rachel : But what if it comes true? What could we do? Wouldn't we just become slaves to our machines, relying entirely on them to do all the things we used to do ourselves?

Mr. Jackson : We certainly need to think about this possibility before we allow it to happen. But I strongly suspect that computers will always be our efficient servants, helping us to accomplish the things we want to do, not the other way around.

Questions

1. In your opinion, will computers soon replace people?
2. What do you think about a robot doing all your work?
3. How could you spend your free time if a machine did everything for you?

Read Me

Being with Someone at a Distance

Are face-to-face communications different than networking on a computer, or are they essentially the same? F2F, of course, has an immediacy that electronic communication does not. We can see, hear, smell, and touch each other in ways that can't be duplicated on a monitor. And it is easier to convey our real message, through gestures and vocal inflections, than it is across the ether. With e-mail or chat rooms, even with the use of emoticons, it's very easy to be misunderstood in terms of our real intent. However, the same criticisms apply to writing letters or talking on the telephone, but that doesn't mean these other means of communication are "inferior" in anyway. What the computer does is make immediate contact possible, cheaply and easily, between people who are widely separated in time and space. And that is very good thing, don't you think?

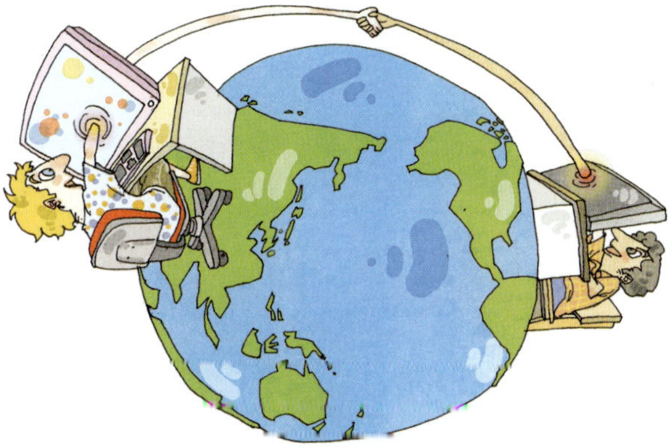

Distance doesn't exist anymore.

Questions

1. What does F2F mean?
2. What are the advantages of personal contact?
3. In what ways is writing a letter better than writing an email? How is talking on the phone better than chatting on a computer?

LIS KOREA에서 나온
DISCUSSION TEXTBOOK

LIS KOREA는 토론 학습 교재 전문 출판사 입니다.

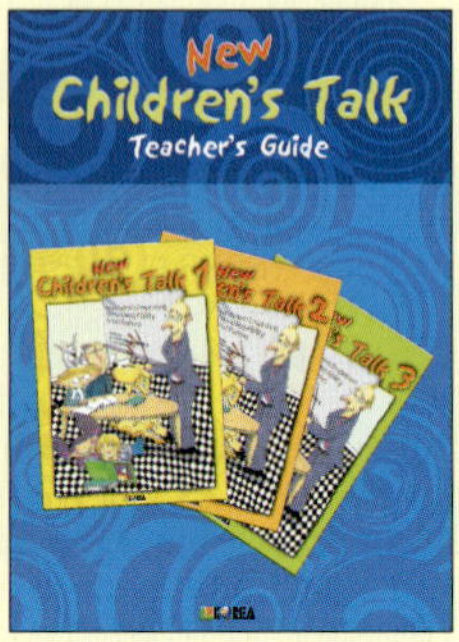

중고급 어린이 들을 위한 독창적인 영어교재

New Children's Talk (1), (2), (3)

교사용

New Children's Talk (TG)

- 일상생활에서 벌어지는 상황들을 다양한 포멧에 맞추어서 많은 Speaking Chance 를 제공합니다.
- 암기위주의 영어가 아니라 자기의견을 만들어 낼 수 있는 포멧들을 제공합니다.

청소년을 위한 토론교재

TEEN TALK (1) (2)

- 각 권 20개의 청소년을 위한 토론 주제 선정
- 영어 표현훈련을 위한 56개의 What-Does-It-Mean Quizzes
- 이해력 향상을 위한 55개의 Comprehension Questions
- 본격적인 토론 훈련을 위한 165개의 Discussion Points
- 자기 의견 형성에 도움을 줄 수 있는 43개의 Opinion Samples
- 독해력 향상을 위한 20개의 Reading Practice를 제공합니다.

중급자들을 위한 토론교재

SPEAK YOUR MIND (1) (2)

- 일상적이며 쉬운 주제들을 선정하여 간결하게 정리했슴.
- 대표 주제에 대한 질문과 대답을 여론조사 형식으로 꾸며 독자들이 쉽게 주제에 접근할 수 있도록 했슴.
- 모든 주제들에 찬반의견을 달아 독자들의 다양한 의견을 접할 수 있도록 했슴.

Chat Room for Teens 2

초판 2쇄 인쇄 : 2010년 1월 5일 인쇄
초판 2쇄 발행 : 2010년 1월 10일 발행
지 은 이 : 리스코리아 편집부 & Duane Vorhees
일러스트레이터 : 김기환
편 집 디 자 인 : 예림칼라
펴 낸 곳 : (도서출판) 리스코리아
펴 낸 이 : 최승신
등 록 : 경기 남양주 제 17호
전 화 : (0502) 423-7947
팩 스 : (0502) 423-7948

www.liskorea.co.kr